Writing with a Point

Ann Harper
Jeanne B. Stephens

Educators Publishing Service, Inc.
Cambridge and Toronto

This book was developed by Ann Harper and Jeanne B. Stephens when they were members of the English Department, Phillips Academy, Andover, Massachusetts.

Contents

1. Brainstorm and Observe

"My paragraph is due tomorrow morning and I haven't written a word!" "What can I write about?" "I don't have anything to say."

In the following pages you will learn how to find something to say by brainstorming and by observing. **Brainstorming** helps you to discover ideas and information that you have stored in your memory; **observing** helps you to discover details that you may not have noticed before. Both techniques can overcome the frustration you may feel when faced with a blank page and an approaching deadline.

Brainstorming

Suppose your teacher asks you to write a paragraph for homework and suggests the general topic "popular entertainment." Because a paragraph should focus on and develop only one main idea, the topic "popular entertainment" is probably too broad to cover adequately in a single paragraph. Thus you will have to narrow the topic first, and find a subtopic of popular entertainment that seems more manageable. Brainstorming is a good way to narrow the topic. Brainstorming is simply the process of writing down ideas that you associate with a particular subject. If you wish to narrow the topic "popular entertainment," for example, you could begin by writing down *types* of popular entertainment, like "rock concerts," "plays," "movies," and "television." These four topics are still very broad, so you could choose one of them and brainstorm again. If you choose the topic "movies," for example, you might come up with the subtopics "recent box-office smashes," "classics," and "foreign films." Suppose you are most interested in the subtopic "recent box-office smashes." That is certainly a more limited topic than popular entertainment, but it is still a fairly general term that encompasses a wide variety of films. Thus you might brainstorm once more, and list "horror films," "adventure films," "teen films," and "high-tech science fiction films."

Here is a chart that illustrates the process of brainstorming to narrow a topic:

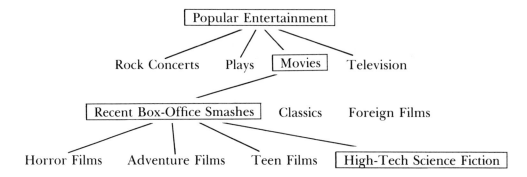

Suppose you choose the topic "high-tech science fiction films." It seems to be a narrow enough topic for a paragraph, but merely deciding on a topic does not mean that you are ready to begin writing. The next step is to discover what you would like to say *about* your topic. Once again, brainstorming can help. This time you are not trying to find subtopics in order to narrow a subject; instead you want to discover what you know about a subject. Thus you would write down all the ideas that come to your mind when you think about "high-tech science fiction."

High-Tech Science Fiction

Star Wars	escapist entertainment
fantasy	adventure, excitement
unrealistic	superhuman control
good always triumphs over evil	futuristic technology

Although these items all deal with the topic of high-tech science fiction, they are not closely related to one another. A paragraph containing all these pieces of information would confuse the reader. Therefore, before you start to write, see if any of the items in your list are related to one another. For example, the three items "good triumphs over evil," "superhuman control," and "futuristic technology" all suggest *how* these films are unrealistic. You could brainstorm again to discover more ideas on this specific angle. You might consider elements like character, plot, setting, and theme, or you might prompt yourself with questions journalists ask when they are writing a story: "who, what, where, when, and why?"

Lack of Realism

characters are like cartoon figures—purely good or purely bad, as in fairy tales or comic books
good always wins

struggles are clear-cut; hero must destroy villain, who has diabolic power
and is trying to take over the world

hero has incredible technological control, sometimes even supernatural
control ("The Force"); battles are filled with dazzling special effects
(lasers, etc.)

space-age setting, props, costumes, etc.

These five items are much more closely related to one another than the ideas on the first list. Now that you have found a specific angle (lack of realism) on a specific topic (high-tech science fiction movies) and have brainstormed some details that are closely related to one another, you are ready to think of a single statement that sums up some of your ideas and makes an interesting point about the topic. This sentence will serve as the foundation of your paragraph.

Here are three possibilities:

1. Recent high-tech science fiction movies resemble fairy-tales and fables, with characters who are either arch-villains or superheroes.
2. Haunted by the threat of nuclear catastrophe, people go to high-tech science fiction movies to see superheroes use sophisticated technology and supernatural forces to defend the world against evil.
3. People flock to science fiction movies because these movies present exciting, unrealistic adventures that present no moral dilemmas—no shades of gray—to complicate the simple story line or to disrupt the happy ending.

Once you have decided on a sentence that sums up the main point of your paragraph, brainstorm a final time to discover some concrete details that could be used to support this particular idea.

Review

Whenever you face a blank page, try collecting your ideas by brainstorming a list of topics that interest you. Then choose one topic and brainstorm subtopics until you have found one that seems narrow enough to write a paragraph about. Brainstorm again, this time not to narrow but to expand. Write down as much information as you can. Then look for connections among the items on your list to see if you can discover a specific angle, or specific point. Express that point in a single sentence. This sentence is called the **point sentence**, because it expresses the main point of your paragraph, the foundation on which you will build. Brainstorm one last time to collect specific details that will illustrate your point sentence.

Exercise ━━

As a class, choose a different subtopic of popular entertainment (page 2) and go through the process described above. Finish by writing several different point sentences.

Exercise ━━

Brainstorm at least six subtopics on the general topic of "television." One subtopic is given as an example.

```
                        ┌────────────┐
                        │ Television │
                        └────────────┘

  Crime dramas
```

Choose a subtopic of television to write about: _____. Now brainstorm again, collecting ideas on this new topic.

_____

_____

_____

_____

_____

_____

Which of these ideas do you find most interesting? Circle them, and brainstorm again on the circled items. List at least seven pieces of information.

_____

_____

_____

_____

_____

_____

Look at the ideas you've listed, and see whether you can make some connections among them. Ask yourself questions like "How? Why? So what? Why is this important?" Can you discover a main idea? Write one below:

_____

_____

_____

_____

_____

Now that you have a main point, brainstorm for the final time, collecting as many ideas and details as you can to illustrate and support this point sentence. Your teacher may ask you to write a paragraph using this point sentence and these details.

_____

_____

_____

_____

_____

_____

_____

"Real Life" Brainstorming

The sample brainstorming on high-tech science fiction movies (page 2) was simplified for the sake of clarity. In real life, however, thinking is usually confused and complex. You will rarely brainstorm without false starts, digressions, and detours. Therefore, try to enjoy the unpredictable process of circling closer to one main conclusion. Brainstorming will help most if you let your thoughts roam, if you give yourself the space and time to travel down a few roads even though they may turn out to be dead ends. Be patient. The process of elimination is a good technique for discovering what you have to say.

Read through the model below, taken from a "real-life" classroom. The students began by brainstorming to narrow the broad topic "relationships."

Relationships

parent-child	siblings	(school friends)
neighbors	teacher-student	marriage
divorce	employee-employer	coach-team
minister-congregation	step-parent and child	boy-girl

School Friends

friends from same grade	homeroom friends	friends on sports teams
friends in extracurricular activities	(cliques)	boy-girl friends
	boyfriend-girlfriend	

The class chose "cliques" as a topic suitable in scope—not too broad and not too narrow—for a paragraph. Then they brainstormed for ideas on this topic. Notice that when the ideas are written down, they are not parallel in structure. For example, some are phrases, while others are clauses and full sentences. When you brainstorm, do not stop to correct or change your writing. Simply jot down all the ideas that occur to you.

Cliques
    hurt of exclusion
    cliques lead to stereotyping of both insiders and outsiders
    cliques seem self-confident, yet individual members may lack confidence
    destroys other relationships: limits number of people you can become close to
    clique gets identity from outsiders, who label it, as much as from insiders
    pressure to be the same: members adopt similar clothes, attitudes, habits, "style"
    if you don't conform, you could be excluded
    members don't have individual identity; they get identity from group
    clique provides security, comfort, attention, status, peer approval
    clique breeds dependence: if you're rejected by a clique, you lose identity, security, status, etc.
    people in cliques don't necessarily know one another very well or even like one another
    both boys and girls have cliques—not a masculine or feminine issue
    cliques have "personalities": artsy, preppy, druggie, racial or ethnic group, punks, "the beautiful people," the "popular crowd," jocks, "freaks," "geeks," etc.
    "floaters" don't belong to cliques; they have the self-confidence to have friends in many different kinds of groups; do not need to be identified with any one clique
    jealousy
    "contagion theory": "If I'm friends with him, I'll be popular, too."
    "herd" instinct; everyone follows
    security is false; if you make a mistake, you're out
    you don't necessarily know you're in a clique; *you* might think you're open-minded, but others might not perceive you that way
    cliques make superficial, sometimes cruel judgments of outsiders
    false sense of superiority: "ins" vs. "outs"

CATEGORIES

The class couldn't possibly have included all, or even most, of the points above. If they had tried, their paragraphs would have been far too long and confusing. To decide the main point they wanted to make about cliques, they next asked themselves which ideas went together, or fit in categories. Putting ideas into categories—in other words, grouping similar ideas together—will help you "take stock of your inventory." You will discover what kind of information you have, and how much of it there is.

Reasons People Want to be in Cliques
    security
    acceptance by peers—popularity
    you're given an identity—you don't have to figure out who you are or
        how you should act
    you have friends who are like you, who share your interests
    status, attention
    ready-made friends

Types of Cliques
    artsy—theatre people, musicians, artists
    sports cliques—jocks
    "the beautiful people"
    preppies
    the "drug crowd"
    cliques based on race or ethnic group
    punks
    "geeks" or "nerds"

How Cliques Are Destructive
    exclusive—outsiders can feel rejected, inferior
    they breed false sense of superiority; "ins" vs. "outs"
    encourage superficial, often critical, stereotyped judgment of outsiders
    pressure to conform, to have similar appearance, attitudes, habits, "style"
    pressure to do what clique does, even if you disagree, like drinking or
        taking drugs, or being snobbish to others
    you can cut yourself off from people who might have become good friends
    you become dependent on clique for identity, confidence, thoughts
    they can raise false hopes—"If I could join the cheerleader clique, I could
        be popular"
    friendships within the clique might be superficial, based on clique mem-
        bership rather than on understanding and genuine affection for one
        another
    fear of being rejected by clique for making wrong move, liking the "wrong"
        kind of person

Identity
    sometimes identity comes from outsiders, not necessarily insiders
    "I like them individually, but I hate them as a group."
    members of clique have little individual identity—their identity comes
        from the group
    "contagion theory": "If I'm friends with him and in his clique, then I'll
        be popular, self-confident, cool, too."
    pressure to conform, fit in with group identity—embarrassing and threat-
        ening to be different

Dividing your brainstormed list into categories not only helps you see what kind of information you have; it can also lead you to *new* information, because you make connections between ideas as you group them. After they had categorized, the class tried to express some conclusions in one-sentence statements—**point sentences**. Each of the point sentences could serve as the foundation of a paragraph.

Notice that #1 below comes from the category "Reasons people want to be in cliques"; #2 from the category "Identity"; and #3 from the category "How cliques are destructive."

POSSIBLE POINT SENTENCES

1. Cliques offer people security by giving them both a sense of belonging and a group of ready-made friends.
2. In trying to assume an acceptable and comfortable identity by joining a clique, teenagers may lose much of their individual identities.
3. Because cliques are based on distinctions between those who are "in" and those who are "out," they breed a false sense of superiority that is destructive to both insiders and outsiders.

Exercise

Look at the brainstormed details and the categories again. Write a point sentence of your own on the topic of cliques.

_____

_____

_____

Exercise

For homework, brainstorm one of the following topics: sports, boy-girl relationships, clothes. Narrow the topic you've chosen by brainstorming subtopics. Choose one subtopic and brainstorm again. Next, divide your list into categories. Then try to express three interesting conclusions, each in one sentence.

Observing

Brainstorming is a method for discovering and unearthing all that you already know about a subject. In a sense, you are letting down a line into your brain and "fishing" for ideas. **Observing**, on the other hand, is a process of looking *outward*, not delving inward. When you observe, you use all your senses to notice as much as you can. As with brainstorming, you write down as many details and ideas as possible, without pausing to censor, correct, or change anything.

Observing things in the world around you provides one of the best sources of information for writing. The key to good writing often lies in the quality of your observations, their depth and precision. To write a paragraph based on direct observation, try imitating the following exercise.

First the writer spent an hour in a local Burger King restaurant describing as concretely as possible whatever she saw, heard, or sensed.

List of Specific Details

Charcoal smell in air. Sign on outside door: "No Bare Feet. Shirts Required. No Pets." Floor made of modern brick-red tiles; shiny brass drain for hosing down floor. Ceiling made of modern white tiles with a few built-in fluorescent light squares. Old-fashioned lamps with brass fittings and translucent white globes hanging from ceiling.

Seating areas compartmentalized to create private eating spaces. Partitions made of glass panels frosted with tulip designs, pine stained to look like oak, and brass fittings. Plastic tables with wood-grain veneer; curved benches of wooden slats like park benches; black steel rods welded to floor supporting the unmovable, functional furniture.

Short curtain of heavy coral fabric with drapery pleats over main window. Artificial plants in brass pots and planters lined up regularly along hanging mauve shelves. Two pictures on wall—colored pen and ink drawings of restful nature scenes. Frames stained like oak. Small-print wallpaper of tiny coral flowers on delicate vines against a white background.

Self-serve salad bar surrounded by sneeze guards; two bouquets of artificial flowers on the side and a basket of artificial fruit on top. "One serving, please" written on circular handmade sign taped to sneeze guard. Self-serve drinks bar offers coffee, tea, and soft drinks. Sign: "Soda Dispensing Easier if Ice Drawn First; Ice Located in These Dispensers."

Recessed garbage cans—no mention of "trash"; built in "Thank You" signs on push-tops. Bathrooms not visible. Baby's high chair made of brown, molded plastic with white plastic tray and seat belt. Silverware is packaged in plastic.

Customers range in age; most seem upscale. One family includes man wearing baseball cap and green flannel shirt, jeans with keys at belt, sunglasses, moustache; woman in camel coat with baby in pink snow suit. Waitress with gray hair in rust-colored polyester uniform with rust polyester pants and casual shoes. Uniform top is one-piece, made to look like two: checked yellow blouse with Peter Pan collar underneath a rust tunic. Mopping and cleaning, she swoops down on booths and tables as soon as people leave. Custodian with long broom sweeps floor.

Large order board with three sections flanked by "King Combo" pictures and prices. "Chicken—all white meat $1.85;" "Whaler fish fillet $1.35;" "Salad in bowl (with any sandwich purchase/one serving please) $1.39;" "Croissan'wich."

Brass handrail guides line for people waiting to order. Voice of woman behind counter: "Coffee is around the corner. Help yourself. Have a nice day." Sound of numbers being called out for orders.

Signs in striking colors throughout the restaurant: "Pick up Order here" "Please Order Here" "Please Present Coupon before Order" "$150 in Ski Lift Discounts for 15 Cents." Cardboard mobile suspended above counter says, "Go Ahead! Treat yourself to a Winner! Whopper. Croissan'wich for Breakfast!" Cardboard notices, mini-placards on tables: "Cherry Pie. Delicious."

CATEGORIES

Next the writer tried to group the details into categories that represented general impressions.

1. Artificiality: from the décor to the furniture to the employees' uniforms. (brick-looking tiles, wood-grain veneer tables; uniforms; plastic plants and flowers; all wood stained to look like oak.)
2. Genteel décor: striving to be more upscale than a Burger King is expected to be. (old-fashioned lamps; elaborate partitions with frosted glass; tiny floral prints on wallpaper; curtain suggesting a drapery; recessed wastebaskets and inconspicuous bathrooms.)
3. Efficiency and cleanliness: from the layout of the restaurant (especially the separation of the ordering section from the seating section) to the clean-up by employees. (self-service salad and drinks bar; shiny metal drain for hosing; waitress swooping down to wipe tables.)

Preliminary Conclusion

Then the writer connected the ideas of artificiality, genteel décor, and efficiency to form one conclusion:

> Burger King's décor is designed to make customers forget that they are in a fast-food restaurant by covering a functional core with "genteel" decorative touches.

Next she went back to her list of details and collected the ones that illustrated the first part of her statement:

> Functional, fast-food core: brick-like floor with drain for hosing; black steel rods welded to floor to support tables and chairs; waitresses cleaning quickly and frequently; fluorescent lights in ceiling; baby's plastic high chair; numbers called out for orders; signs everywhere.

Exercise

Collect details to illustrate the second part of the conclusion by circling those that fit into the category of "genteel décor."

The writer could use these details to develop an interesting paragraph about Burger King's decor. However, if the writer wishes to go one step further, she could consider the significance of her conclusion. *Why* might Burger King be designed this way? This last step could yield an even more developed point:

> Burger King is "trying harder" because it is number two after MacDonald's, which is secure in its fast-food identity and success. Burger King is striving to capture more of the market by upgrading its basic fast-food image.

MODEL PARAGRAPH

Burger King is "trying harder" to capture more of the fast-food market by attracting upscale customers. The minute they step inside the front door, Burger King patrons can see that this is not the usual fast-food place, but a restaurant striving to create a genteel atmosphere while it delivers fast food with efficiency and cleanliness. The honor system operates at the salad bar, where customers help themselves, policed only by a homemade sign saying "One Serving, Please." This gracious "help yourself" attitude also prevails at the drink bar, where patrons pay a clerk, who gives them an empty cup which they can then fill with ice and the drink of their choice. Settling into curved, slatted benches, patrons can enjoy their own private dining area separated from the noise of fellow diners by elaborate partitions of frosted glass and brass fittings. House plants on hanging mauve shelves, restful pen and ink scenes, and tasteful wallpaper with tiny coral flowers on delicate vines decorate the walls. Yet underneath these decorator touches lies the functional core of a fast-food restaurant. Above the old-fashioned lamps, whose brass fittings are purely decorative, is a fully functional ceiling of white tiles and fluorescent squares. The cozy curved benches are held in place by black steel rods welded to the floor. In the center of the brick-look floor tiles is a shiny metal drain which makes hosing down the restaurant quick and easy. In surroundings where even the wastebaskets are discreetly hidden under "Thank You"'s, Burger King's customers may soon make it the true king of the fast-food business.

Exercise

1. What is the main point of the paragraph?

_____

_____

_____

2. Put two lines under any sentence or phrase in the paragraph that repeats its main conclusion in different words. How many sentences echo the point in some form?
3. Go back and put one line under any detail in the original list that is mentioned in the paragraph. Be ready to explain *how* the writer has used each detail to support the main conclusion of the paragraph.
4. How might you use some of the other details in the original list to support the main point?

Review

When your teacher asks your class to write about something that you are to observe, remember that you will all be looking at the same subject—whether a place, person, or picture—but you will see different details. Good writers look closely, and try to interpret imaginatively what they see.

Exercise

First day

1. Your class brainstorms places to write about and then decides on one.
2. Each of you makes a list of twenty to thirty important details that you observe at the place.
3. Review the list of details, starring or circling the most important ones and adding more description to the starred items. (Example: "radiator" becomes "peeling, cracked, forlorn radiator.")
4. Look for a dominant impression and write a preliminary conclusion in one sentence. Your teacher will check these.
5. For homework, write a paragraph that uses plenty of details to support your conclusion.

Second day

1. In groups of two or three, read one another's paragraphs. Ask a partner to comment on the dominant impression of the paragraph and the concreteness of its details.
2. For homework, revise your draft to respond to your partner's suggestions.

Third day

1. In groups of three, choose the best paragraph. Then your teacher will read each group's choice aloud. As a class, discuss the best paragraphs. What makes them so effective?

Exercise

From your memory write a paragraph about a place that made an impact on you as a child—for example, a grade-school classroom, playground, or your grandparents' house. Remember to select details carefully, making sure that they are as concrete and specific as possible. All your details should contribute to one dominant impression. Use a good point sentence to give a focus to your information.

2. Categorize

To help you write better paragraphs, this workbook divides the writing process into four main steps:

1. Brainstorm and/or observe to collect ideas and information;
2. Categorize information to discover preliminary conclusions;
3. Write a point sentence that expresses the main idea of the paragraph;
4. Develop the paragraph by selecting and ordering details that support its point sentence.

In the preceding pages you practiced the first step of the process, brainstorming and observing. In the pages that follow, you will master each of the remaining steps. By concentrating on each skill, you can learn how to write paragraphs that interest and involve your readers.

Creating Categories

As you fill a page with brainstormed ideas, you will discover what you know about a topic. But before you can draw a significant conclusion, you will need to categorize your list of details. Categorizing means putting together things that have something in common. Thinking of headings for each category will help you to begin to make the connections that will suggest a focus for your paragraph.

In the Burger King model, for example, the writer first sorted details simply by their place in the restaurant: one category contained everything she observed near the counter; another category contained everything near the seating area. This type of categorizing is the simplest. Next the writer tried to discover less obvious similarities. Noting that many objects in the restaurant were artificial, she made a category for "artificiality." The more probing your categories, the sharper your final conclusion is likely to become.

MODEL: SCHOOL SPORTS

The random subtopics below were discovered by brainstorming on the topic "school sports."

soccer	ice hockey	swimming
football	baseball	wrestling

softball	gymnastics	track
tennis	basketball	volleyball
field hockey		

Then the writer placed the subtopics in categories that revealed similarities. (The groupings were made on the basis of traditional divisions in competitive sports.)

Boys' Sports	Girls' Sports	Both Genders
football	field hockey	soccer
wrestling	softball	gymnastics
baseball	volleyball	track
ice hockey		basketball
		swimming
		tennis

Contact	Non-contact
football	soccer
wrestling	gymnastics
ice hockey	track
	basketball
	field hockey
	swimming
	softball
	baseball
	tennis
	volleyball

Based on gender and contact, these are only two groups of categories. There are many others.

Exercise

Can you think of other groups of categories? List some. Don't worry if some items fall into more than one category, and don't worry if an item does not fit easily into any category. Pay close attention to such misfits; sometimes they lead to particularly interesting conclusions.

Exercise

Suppose you are going to write a paragraph about cigarette smoking. As the first step, you've brainstormed the following list. To see how much and what kind of information you have, put these items into several categories. If any one category seems too big, try breaking it down into smaller groups. Use the space on the next page.

smoking is enjoyable
difficult to give up
smoking is a personal freedom

"second hand smoke" is dangerous—passive smoker suffers from smoke
expensive habit
smoke permeates room, clothes of other people
smoker has smelly breath, smelly clothes, smelly hair
discolors teeth
annoying
makes people cough, some people's eyes water
increases chance of lung cancer greatly
increases chance of other lung diseases, like emphysema
increases chance of heart attack, heart disease
increases nation's health care costs
⅕ of all U.S. deaths traced to smoking each year
separate smoking sections in restaurants, on planes
"no smoking" signs in more and more places
smoking cuts appetite—if you quit, you might gain weight
nicotine is addictive
sociable to share a cigarette with someone

————————————————————————
————————————————————————
————————————————————————
————————————————————————
————————————————————————
————————————————————————
————————————————————————
————————————————————————
————————————————————————
————————————————————————
————————————————————————
————————————————————————
————————————————————————
————————————————————————
————————————————————————
————————————————————————
————————————————————————
————————————————————————

Exercise

After categorizing this information, write three different point sentences
that draw a conclusion about the issue of smoking. Then choose one of the
point sentences and write a paragraph that supports it, using some of the
details from the list.

Exercise ━━

Suppose you wanted to write a paragraph on Britain's controversial program for drug addicts: to combat crime and to decrease drug-related deaths, National Health clinics (clinics established by the government) make heroin legally available to addicts. The list below is the result of brainstorming. Categorize it into "pro" and "con" and then see if you can break those broad categories down further.

British have been following this policy since the 1920s.

Addicts don't turn to pimping, prostitution, mugging, burglary, theft.

National Health maintains the addiction—doctor injects at the clinic.

Addicts are advised, not pressured or lectured.

No attempt is made to shame, humiliate, publish names.

Addicts might supplement the dose they receive with heroin obtained on black market.

Syndicated crime has less power, less business.

Society seems to allow, to condone addictive drug use—wrong message.

Why should citizens subsidize junkies (through taxes to the National Health)?

Policy solves the larger social problem of street crime: junkie, pusher, traffickers, money-launderers—whole sub-culture that preys upon innocent people.

Less overdosing: drug is regulated so "purer"; needles aren't shared so AIDS doesn't spread, infecting non-drug users through prostitutes.

Should heroin be available to minors? Where does one draw the line? Would the policy broaden the population of users? Since there's no penalty like jail for using heroin and since it's free and available, wouldn't more people try it? No deterrence through jail, high expense, or danger.

The troubles of the families of addicts wouldn't be solved: they'd still have a person who couldn't function.

Black market would not be eradicated—still supplies other drugs and heroin to those who choose not to go to National Health clinics and be identified.

Pro	Con

Smaller Categories (List them.)

_____
_____
_____
_____
_____
_____
_____
_____
_____
_____
_____

Exercise

After you have categorized this information, write three different point sentences, arguing different points of view. Choose one of the point sentences, and write a paragraph defending it.

_____
_____
_____
_____
_____
_____
_____
_____
_____
_____
_____
_____

Exercise

Choose a topic to brainstorm. With one person at the blackboard as recorder, brainstorm on the topic for ten to fifteen minutes. Then sort your information into categories.

MODEL: OLYMPICS

As you read the model below, note how important the step of categorizing is. The writer first brainstormed the following list on the topic of the Olympics.

amateur sports (supposedly)
Olympic torch
flag with circles interlocking
commercialism
nationalism—patriotism vs. prejudice
competition, individual and team
boycotts due to politics (by Soviets in 1984; Americans in 1980)
PLO terrorist attack on Israeli athletes (Munich, 1972)
corruption—steroids, drugs
medal count—the charts
pursuit of excellence
America "lost" in Montreal (1976)
George Orwell's line: "International sport is war without shooting."

Next the writer categorized these details to narrow her focus and to develop one significant conclusion.

Symbols	Positive elements of Olympics
Olympic torch	amateur sports
flag with circles	patriotism, unity of spirit
medal count—charts	competition of individuals and teams
	pursuit of excellence

Negative elements
amateur competition, supposedly, but some athletes are paid by their governments
nationalism becomes chauvinism and prejudice—divisive
politics interfere
boycotts
terrorist attacks
corruption—drugs
medal count
America "lost"
Orwell's line

Next the writer examined her categories more closely and discovered that under "negative elements," the term "politics" actually covered many other items in that list. In fact, if she omitted "commercialism" and "corruption," the remaining items all suggested *how* the politics of the Olympic Games create negative effects. Thus, the process of categorizing led the writer to consider a preliminary conclusion: although the Olympics has some positive characteristics, politics undercuts them. The writer then pursued this idea by brainstorming again to expand on her original ideas.

The positive elements

- the pursuit of excellence: athlete in competition with himself or herself, testing discipline, strength, and competence
- unity and friendship: nations gathered together in peace, with a common goal, to excel

- patriotism: pride one feels when one's country's flag is raised and anthem is played

The negative elements

- medal count: who "won" and who "lost"
- individual or team victory becomes victory for the country and its way of life (flag raised, anthem played—that country won, not the athlete)
- patriotism can encourage prejudice: divides more than it unites
- world-wide attention makes Olympic Games a stage for terrorism (PLO attack) and for political acts (two boycotts and exclusion of South Africa because of apartheid)
- Orwell's "war without shooting": competition can be destructive to international friendship and understanding

Just before starting her paragraph, the writer used a brief outline to put the information into an orderly pattern.

I. Positive elements
   A. For the individual: the pursuit of excellence symbolized by Olympic torch
   B. For the team, country, potentially the world: unity and friendship symbolized by flag with interlocking circles
II. Negative elements created by politics
   A. Overtly political actions like terrorism and boycotts
   B. More subtle political actions like medal counts that tell which countries "won" and "lost"; individual athletes and teams are forgotten; pits country against country
   C. Victory for athlete becomes victory for country and its way of life.
   D. Patriotism becomes nationalistic prejudice.

Conclusion: Orwell's statement

Exercise ──

In the model paragraph on Olympics below, insert the Roman numeral or capital letter from the outline above wherever the idea that it represents is introduced. The first three have already been inserted.

Although we tend to glorify the Olympics as a noble competition for

amateur athletes from around the world, the Games are, in fact, highly—

I.

even dangerously—political. Images from the Games reflect this idealism

A.

as well as this realism. The image of the Olympic torch proudly held high

suggests the solitary and dedicated pursuit of excellence by individual ath-

B.

letes. Similarly, the Olympic flag with its five interlocking circles suggests the tantalizing possibility of unity and friendship within the community of nations. But other images cast a menacing shadow on these idealized visions. The image of Israeli athletes murdered by PLO terrorists reminds us that politically motivated violence can strike the Games at any moment. We have yet another picture of suffering caused by the politicizing of the Games when we recall the deeply disappointed athletes who heard a grim-faced President Carter declare a boycott of the 1980 Moscow Olympics in response to the Soviet invasion of Afghanistan. Four years later history repeated itself when Soviet athletes were barred from the Los Angeles Olympics. Some might argue that these examples are extreme and, hence, unrepresentative of the Games. But we need only point to the tallies of medals won and lost for proof of the more subtle harm the political competitiveness of the Olympics inflicts. Individual athletes and teams are forgotten as each country stockpiles its "wins" as though every medal justified its political system. Thus a win for East Germany or Russia means a win for communism, while a win for America represents a triumph for democracy. Nationalistic pride easily becomes nationalistic prejudice. Long after the image of a particular runner breaking the tape has faded, we remember the charts showing that America "lost" the Montreal Olympics in 1976. As we consider future Olympiads, we should temper our idealizing with these words from George Orwell: "International sport is war without shooting."

Selecting Details

The paragraph below was written from direct observation. Notice the wealth of concrete detail, but the absence of any focusing point.

There are many interesting aspects of malls. Malls offer the shopper a wide range of stores selling one special product: records, jeans, sports equipment, pets, shoes, hosiery, maternity clothes, phones, and tobacco. Large department stores like Sears or Jordan Marsh anchor the ends of malls, while food stands line the corridors, selling chocolate chip cookies, chicken fingers, salads, blond brownies, ice cream, Orange Julius, tacos, egg rolls, Papa Gino's pizza, and Bavarian strudel. Big restaurants like a New York Steak House and a large Italian restaurant post outside their doors color photographs of the meals they offer: "Fresh! honey-glazed roast chicken dinner $3.99," "Cutlets parmigiana," "Broiled scrod." Jewelry stores offer sales: "Save 50% No Money Down," while a cosmetic booth, glassed in like a miniature greenhouse, invites customers to "Treat your face to a personal beauty service." Sometimes a car like a Mustang is raffled off in the mall's center, lined with large, bulbous, street lamps. Security guards with two-way radios walk the malls, while custodians empty waste-bins. Near the specialty stores, there are often dark video-game arcades, lighted only by blinking colored bulbs on game screens. Music is piped into the mall from several directions and a store selling player organs offers a continuous demonstration of their sounds. Young couples walk along with babies in strollers; old men with blank faces sit on park benches or at small tables under transplanted trees. Older women walk side by side carrying several shopping bags with names of stores on them; some wear trench coats, others wear slacks or suits. Teenage boys stride down the avenue laughing and smoking cigarettes. They wear black, punk-rock T-shirts. Teenage girls with layered hair and painted fingernails shop in pairs. Their shoes have high, thick wooden heels. Some men wear overalls, Hawaiian shirts, or three-piece, seersucker suits and roadster caps. Little children carry ice cream cones and stuffed animals bought by grandparents. The parking lots of malls hold hundreds of cars and every day, except Sunday, they are filled. Finally, malls are usually open from 10:00 a.m. until 9:30 in the evening. A large sign on the lot announces, "We're a great place to be, Shop over 100 stores."

The information in this paragraph overwhelms the reader, who wonders what the writer's point could be. To select the appropriate details which illustrate one particular point, first think of some broad categories to put the details into. For example, one category might include items that appeal to one's senses. Fill in the details for this category, and then think of at least three other categories.

Appeal to Senses

_____ (category 2)

_____ (category 3)   _____ (category 4)

Now look at these preliminary categories more closely. Do they raise any questions that might help you to select some details and combine them into new categories?

What is appealing about malls?

- variety of products and pleasures (shop and eat)
- convenience (parking lot; easy access)
- pleasant, safe environment (security guards; park atmosphere)

Here are two point sentences which developed from the categorizing exercise above.

1. The mall offers a wide variety of experiences—bright colors, pleasing sounds, delicious tastes and smells—that stimulate customers and make them feel alive, alert, and cheerful.
2. The mall brainwashes customers, turning them into mindless robots.

Exercise

Write one more point sentence from the mall description. Then write a paragraph supporting either your own point or one taken from the two points above. Select and include in the paragraph only those details that best support your conclusion.

Exercise

Go to the lobby of a local movie theatre. Write down in a list or in paragraph form all the details that you observe. Then categorize your information. On the next day in class, read aloud your details. As a group, categorize the items that everyone has collected and then write two or three point sentences.

3. Write a Point Sentence

You have practiced categorizing details that you've gathered by brainstorming and observing. And you have begun to draw preliminary conclusions by thinking about those categories. But how exactly do you turn a general conclusion into a clear and crisp sentence? This section of the workbook will help you to recognize and to write good point sentences, the third step of the writing process.

From Categories to Point Sentence

Suppose you were going to write on the subject of "faces," and you brainstormed the following list:

acne and acne problems
tanning salons
skin products—billion-dollar industry
dermatologists
beautiful models with perfect skin
diet and exercise
fashion magazines
health
appearance
make-up
sleep—circles under eyes
plastic surgery
lab-coated cosmetics salespeople—pseudo-scientists

To draw some conclusions, you would try to categorize these terms. Two categories that might occur to you are "inner" and "outer": what people apply to their faces to make them look better, such as skin products, acne medication, and make-up; and what people do from the "inside" to improve their skin, such as get more exercise and sleep, or improve their diet. These opposing categories could lead you to the conclusion stated in the point sentence below.

> Instead of modifying their diets and exercise habits to promote healthier skin, Americans prefer to spend billions on skin products and cosmetics.

From List of Terms to Point Sentence

Another way to develop a point sentence is to write a sentence that connects some of the pieces of information. For example, the items "fashion magazine" and "beautiful models with perfect skin" go together, and you could link them with the item "billion-dollar industry in skin products." Try to write a sentence that includes all three phrases by finding some logical connection between them:

"fashion magazines" + "beautiful models" = "billion-dollar industry"

Using the perfect faces of perfect models, monthly fashion magazines manipulate readers into buying billions of dollars of cosmetics.

Similarly, you might link the items "dermatologists" with "lab-coated cosmetics salespeople" and see that the cosmetic companies are trying to make their products seem "scientific" and, therefore, legitimate by dressing their salespeople as dermatologists and by putting "skin computers" on their sales counters. Thus you might write:

The billion-dollar cosmetic industry seeks greater profits by implying that their skin products are as scientifically legitimate as the skin medications provided by dermatologists.

Your goal is, first, to see connections between a few items on your brainstormed list and, then, to sum up those logical connections in one sentence.

Exercise

Connecting different items from the list of details on "faces," write a point sentence of your own.

_____

_____

Exercise

Below are five more lists of brainstormed items. Write two point sentences for each topic by connecting at least two items from each list.

TV Commercials

silly	irresponsible	housewives, macho men
manipulative	sugar-coated cereal	sentimental
repetitive	sexual suggestiveness	competitive market
funny	stereotyping	unfounded claims

_____

_____

_____

Motorcycles

Easy Rider
Hell's Angels
Altamont Rock Concert
symbols of rebellion, an-
  archy and lawlessness
CHIPs, police motorcycles
black leather
Biker magazine
danger

highway driving
invisible to motorists
adolescent initiation
gas mileage
efficiency
mopeds
inexpensive transporta-
  tion

export-import competi-
  tion
Honda vs. Harley-
  Davidson
gangs
helmet laws
American dream: the
  open road

_____

_____

_____

_____

Soap Operas

excitement
glamourous, wealthy lives
violence
stereotypes
passive entertainment

fantasy
beautiful people
melodrama
questionable ethics
common problems—
  divorce, death, sickness

long-running programs
"General Hospital"
popularity among
  women, teens
addiction

_____

_____

_____

_____

_____

Body Building

pumping iron
"athletic activism"
Jane Fonda
Arnold Schwartzenegger,
  Charles Atlas

Nautilus and Universal
  machines
efficient exercise
body building as an art
  form

body building as a sport
women weight lifters
body-building contests—
  beauty shows

_____

_____

_____

_____

_____

_____

<u>Overeating</u>

diets
splurging–guilt–
  depression–cycle
societal pressure to be
  thin
parental pressure
junk food
metabolism changes

guilt–"Clean your plate;
  people are starving."
appetite suppressants
myths about food and
  skin problems (choco-
  late, greasy food)
why do we overeat? to

relax, procrastinate, so-
  cialize
we eat because we hang
  out at fast-food places
eating disorders–bulimia
  (vomit or purge after
  splurging)

_____

_____

_____

_____

_____

_____

Making a Point

Which one of the sentences below would you rather read or write about? Why?

a) _Seventeen_ magazine is a best-selling teen fashion magazine that offers advice on cosmetics, clothes, and behavior.

b) _Seventeen_ magazine may pride itself on fashioning independent, self-assertive young women, but the magazine actually encourages an unhealthy dependence on its "laws" for looking, thinking, and acting "right."

The first sentence states a fact: _Seventeen_ offers advice on clothes, cosmetics, and behavior. It does not, however, show you the significance of that fact. The second sentence makes a point: _Seventeen_ actually encourages an unhealthy dependence, though it seems to be doing the opposite. A paragraph that takes a stand on its topic usually is more interesting both to write and to read. The writer is challenged not simply to gather facts but to interpret them in ways that engage the reader. The reader, in turn, reads something that makes him stop and think.

A Point Sentence Checklist

Writing a sentence that expresses the main point of your paragraph is the third step of the writing process. But not just any sentence will do. When you're stating your point, ask yourself the following questions:

1. Does the point sentence capture your own **interest**? Do you want to write about it?
2. Will the point sentence seem **significant** or important to your reader? Will your reader want to read on?
3. Does the point sentence express a **point of view**, a judgment or an opinion on your topic?
4. Is the point sentence appropriate in **scope**, or is its focus too broad or too narrow?
5. Is the point sentence **clearly stated**? Are its **key terms** precise, or are they vague, general, or overly abstract?
6. If the point sentence has more than one clause, are the parts of the sentence **logically connected**?

Interest

Even though you will often have to write on topics that you haven't chosen and that you may find uninteresting, look for an angle on the topic that you can write about with conviction. If you simply dismiss the assignment as boring, the chances are you will settle for the first ideas—commonplace thoughts and fuzzy generalizations—that come to mind. If, on the other hand, you can choose a topic or find an angle that you care about, you will have an easier time writing an interesting point sentence.

Let's say, for example, that your teacher asks you to write about conservation. At first glance this subject may leave you cold. Yet after some thought, you might remember a lobsterman you know whose livelihood has been threatened by inadequate conservation laws. Because you have seen your friend lose his store and boat as a result of the inaction of state legislators—because you have personal experience of his suffering—you can write a point sentence and paragraph that are interesting not only to you but to others as well. Remember: if your point sentence interests you, you will probably be able to make it interesting to others. But remember also that you must engage the reader; it is not enough simply to interest yourself.

Significance

If a reader asks "So what?" after she finishes your point sentence, you have a problem with significance. Point sentences that make obvious claims or that state commonly known facts prompt the reader to ask why you have told her something that she already knows. Even if you state an unusual or little-known fact, you still need to make its importance clear. For example, if you've written, "In infant mortality the U.S. ranks seventeenth among industrial nations," your reader may think, "This is interesting, but so what? What am I supposed to think about this fact? Why would I want to know this? How is this important? What point is the writer trying to make?" To clarify the significance of the fact, you might suggest *why* it is true: "**The U.S. mis-**

places its money on high-technology heroics to save the lives of tiny, premature babies; the money would be better used to prevent premature births by upgrading programs that give free prenatal care." This point sentence takes a forceful stand on the issue of infant mortality rates and proposes a significant solution.

To make sure that your conclusion will seem significant to your reader, try approaching the topic with any one of these goals in mind:

- to challenge a prevalent stereotype;
- to take a bold stand on a controversial issue;
- to find a new and arresting way of defining something familiar;
- to make an unusual comparison or analogy;
- to propose an original solution to an old problem;
- to claim an unexpected cause-effect relationship between two events;
- to make a judgment based on moral or artistic standards that you set up.

And after you've written a point sentence, test its significance by asking yourself the following questions: "What is important about this fact or idea?" "How do I feel about it?" "What is the effect of this?" "How or why did this happen?" "What should be done about it?"

If you follow these suggestions, you can probably assume that the reader will find your point sentence significant and will be curious to see how you develop and illustrate your point.

Exercise ———————————————————————

Discuss the following point sentences with your class. How might you make them more interesting and more significant to a reader? Rewrite three of them.

1. The growing high-school dropout rate should be a matter of great concern to educators and public officials.
2. Football is responsible for more frequent and more serious injuries than any other sport.
3. Being a middle child in my family is not easy.
4. The growing epidemic of AIDS has led to public hysteria.
5. More Americans are killed each year in alcohol- or drug-related car accidents than were killed during the Vietnam War.

_____

_____

_____

_____

_____

_____

Point of View

Another way to guarantee that your point sentence does, in fact, make a point is to ask yourself whether you've made a judgment or expressed an opinion about the topic. Have you made your attitude, your position clear? The requirement to adopt a point of view does not mean that you should make biased, emotional, or unsupportable statements. There is a difference between being judgmental and making a judgment, between being opinionated and expressing an opinion. Insisting that, "Everyone is entitled to his own opinion; it's a free country," will not persuade a reader to accept an excessive claim. Rather, taking a reasonable stand after considering a topic will help you to sharpen your ideas, and encourage the reader to adopt your point of view.

Exercise

Discuss the following point sentences with your class. How might you improve them by adding or strengthening the writer's point of view? Choose three and revise them.

Example: Prime-time soap operas like "Dynasty" and "Dallas" are completely asinine.

Revised: Prime-time soap operas like "Dynasty" and "Dallas" are morally distasteful because they show viewers that the only things worth caring for are oneself and one's possessions.

1. There are twenty-three million functionally illiterate adults and another thirty-five million semi-literate adults in the United States.
2. Over the past twenty years, verbal and math S.A.T. scores have declined noticeably.
3. The largest audience for movies these days is teenagers, a fact Hollywood is very aware of.
4. My 10:00 p.m. curfew on Saturday night is ridiculous.
5. The policy of apartheid in South Africa legalizes political, economic, and social discrimination against the majority of the population.

_____

_____

_____

_____

_____

_____

_____

_____

Scope

How much ground can you cover in a paragraph without being overly general or excessively detailed? How broad or narrow is your topic? Having a good sense of scope comes with experience. Seasoned writers seem to know by instinct what can be handled well in a paragraph, whereas beginning writers often choose topics that are too broad because they're afraid that they won't find enough to say unless their subject covers a lot of ground. Anxious about the blank page, they make themselves feel safer by quickly choosing a broad topic. Then they throw every general idea and stray detail into a grab-bag paragraph that never has any sharpness because it has been doomed from the start by its overly broad scope.

Although the question of scope is initially a question for the writer alone—each individual writer brings a different amount of knowledge to his or her topic—the reader also makes a judgment about the scope of a paragraph. If your topic is too broad, your reader may find that your treatment is superficial, overly general, or vague; because you have to cover so much, you might be unable to provide real depth in your analysis. Therefore, instead of leaping immediately into a broad topic, spend some time narrowing your subject and discovering what you know about it by brainstorming. Time spent on preliminary thinking and narrowing is never wasted.

If you want to write about "television," for example, you must first narrow the scope of your topic. What element of television are you interested in? Do you want to discuss violence on T.V.? Children's shows? The quality of T.V. movies? Educational programming? Crime dramas? Sitcoms? Soap operas? Evening or morning news programs? Commercials? The effect of television on S.A.T. scores? Even the category "children's shows" is broad, because there are so many different types of children's shows and so many things to say about them. Your purpose is not to write a list of programs or a list of observations, but to illustrate and support a specific point. So you must continue to narrow the topic.

Let's say you choose "toy-based cartoons," those Saturday morning cartoons that draw their heroes and villains from products on toy-store shelves. This topic seems neither too narrow nor too broad for a single paragraph; in other words, it has appropriate scope. After brainstorming on this topic, you could write a point sentence like, "**Cartoons based on toys are designed primarily to market toys, and thus they manipulate and exploit the child viewer.**"

One tip to keep in mind when you are considering scope is to avoid the "list point sentence": "There are many. . . ." This sentence will lead you to write out a mere grocery list of details. For example, if you write "There are many complications in a child's life after his parents divorce," you are setting yourself up to write an undeveloped, disconnected list of complications. Instead, you might write, "**One problem of having divorced parents marry new spouses is that the child inherits an instant set of stepbrothers and stepsisters**

whom she may not know or like, yet with whom she must share a home and parental attention." This more narrowly focused point sentence allows you to concentrate on the specific problem of getting along with a new stepfamily. Your paragraph will most likely be much more detailed, more concrete, and more significant than a paragraph that lists the complications of divorce.

It is not a bad idea to write out a list in paragraph form as a way to discover what you want to say, but you must be sure to rewrite your paragraph once you've decided on your main point.

Exercise

Discuss the following point sentences in class. How could you improve their scope? Revise three of the sentences.

Example: Many students procrastinate for a large variety of reasons.

Revised: Many procrastinators are neither lazy nor unmotivated, but are actually perfectionists, who are so afraid of not excelling that they cannot make their best effort.

1. Computers will revolutionize learning in the next decade.
2. Grades cause more problems than they solve.
3. There are many advantages and disadvantages to using scrimmages as the main way to practice soccer.
4. Teenagers use drugs and alcohol because of peer pressure, curiosity, the need to relieve stress, or the desire to imitate a respected model.
5. There are many different trends in rock 'n roll today, some positive and some negative.

———————————————————————————————

———————————————————————————————

———————————————————————————————

———————————————————————————————

———————————————————————————————

———————————————————————————————

———————————————————————————————

———————————————————————————————

Key Terms

Consider the sentence, "A character in a novel can be morally offensive and yet artistically pleasing." To expand on this idea, the writer first must make sure that he knows exactly what he means by the terms "morally offensive" and "artistically pleasing." These are the **key terms** because they express the meanings that the writer will explore and develop in his paragraph. If the key terms of your point sentence are "fuzzy," neither you nor your reader will know exactly what point you're trying to make. Imprecise words suggest at best that you haven't clearly thought through your ideas, at worst that you do not have a point at all.

Beginning writers use three kinds of imprecise key terms. First, they rely on vague, blanket terms such as "aspect," "factor," "thing," "situation," and "condition." These *abstract and general nouns* do little more than hold a place in a sentence, a place that should be filled by a more precise and substantial term. Second, beginning writers rely on *broad and debatable terms* such as "realistic," "romantic," "freedom," "responsibility," "culture," "democracy," "communism," and "society." These terms invite confusion because their definitions are so difficult to pin down. When a writer uses such terms, he often is fleeing to a level of broad generality because ignorance or haste or fear of thinking prevents him from pitching his ideas at a more concrete and specific level. Finally, beginning writers sometimes express *vague judgments* with adjectives like "good," "bad," "better," "best," and "worst." These words are so general that they obscure rather than clarify the basis for judgment. Often they create point sentences that cannot be supported or developed.

Exercise

Put boxes around vague or confusing key terms in the following sentences. Revise three of the sentences.

1. Because of various influences, the government sometimes seems incapable of making laws regarding significant domestic policy.
2. Although the space program has had many problems, it will come back when it makes administrative changes and begins new projects.
3. Learning to formulate proposals for faculty action, students who participate actively in student government can learn how to be politically effective.
4. The welfare system is harmful.
5. Drugs will be an important aspect of any child's life today; therefore, it is important that the child is told when very young the dangers of drug use.
6. Playing on varsity or junior-varsity teams makes people stronger, better, and smarter.

_____

_____

_____

_____

_____

_____

_____

_____

Logical Connections

Now that you have learned the broader requirements for a good point sentence, you can polish that sentence by improving its structure. *Sentence structure* refers both to the groups of words that represent ideas in a sentence and to their relationship to one another. *Clauses*, those groups of words that contain both a subject and a verb, should express ideas that you wish to emphasize. *Phrases*, those groups of words that do not contain both a subject and a verb, tell us something about the clauses. Connecting words such as *prepositions* and *conjunctions* join clauses and phrases to each other in ways that reveal their relative importance in the whole sentence. To improve your sentence structure, make sure that you:

1. express your main idea in the main clause (The main clause can be a sentence by itself.);
2. put qualifying ideas into phrases or subordinate clauses (The subordinate clause cannot be a sentence by itself.); and
3. use conjunctions that show most clearly how each of your ideas relates to every other idea in the sentence.

PUT MAIN IDEAS INTO MAIN CLAUSES.

Notice that an idea placed in a main clause will receive greater emphasis than an idea placed in a subordinate clause. Compare the following sentences.

Even though Kate can't cook an egg, she can understand calculus.

The writer of the first sentence, by placing "she can't cook an egg" in the main clause, implies that no amount of mathematical talent will make up for Kate's failure to cook. On the other hand, the writer of the second sentence, by placing "she can understand calculus" in the main clause, implies that Kate's achievement in higher mathematics more than offsets her dismal cooking. After you decide which idea you want to stress in your point sentence, place that idea into the main clause.

Exercise

Combine each of the following pairs of sentences in at least two ways to vary emphasis and meaning. You may change verb tenses.

Example: Oscar failed his biology final. Oscar stayed up all night smoking dope.

Combinations: Because Oscar failed his biology final, he stayed up all night smoking dope.

After Oscar stayed up all night smoking dope, he failed his biology final.

If Oscar fails his biology final, he will stay up all night smoking dope.

1. Half the class failed the math exam. Everyone had worked diligently all term.

_____

_____

2. Susie broke up with John. John began to drink heavily.

_____

_____

3. Terry's grades improved dramatically. Her self-confidence increased.

_____

_____

PUT QUALIFYING IDEAS INTO PHRASES OR SUBORDINATE CLAUSES.

Compare the following sentences.

The bus was late and he missed his job interview.
Because the bus was late, he missed his job interview.

In the first sentence, *and* functions merely as a plus sign: x + y. In the second sentence, *because* tells the reader that these two ideas are related as cause and effect. The more precisely you can identify the relationships between the ideas in your point sentences, the clearer your thought will be.

USE CONJUNCTIONS THAT SHOW THE LOGICAL CONNECTIONS BETWEEN YOUR IDEAS.

To join subordinate clauses to main clauses, use one of the following connecting words, each of which answers a particular question.

why?	*because* we didn't like eggplant
how?	*as if* he were too busy
	as though she didn't know the truth
in spite of what? . . .	*although* we were still hungry
	even though we wanted a pizza
	though we had already eaten

for what purpose? . .	*so that* the students could pay
under what conditions?	*if* they have enough money
except what?	*unless* the pizza place won't deliver
compared with what?	*more than* we could afford
when?	*after* we had eaten dinner *whenever* we're hungry *until* they get home *while* we waited and waited *before* we went to bed
where?	*where* the roads intersect *wherever* students study late

Try to establish logical relationships between the ideas in your point sentence by using connecting words precisely. Pay particularly close attention to *because*; it should be used only if there is a genuine causal relationship between your ideas.

Wrong: Because school ended in late June, I spent the summer doing odd jobs in the neighborhood.

Revised: Because school ended in late June, I had trouble finding a well-paying summer job that hadn't been taken by college students, who finished school in early May.

Exercise

Rewrite the following sentences to remove *and*. Put the main idea in the main clause; use subordinate clauses and phrases to subordinate all other information to your main clause.

1. There is a shortage of math and science teachers, and math and science majors graduate from college and go into well-paid jobs in business.

   _____

   _____

   _____

2. The public is confused about the U.S.'s role in Central America, and those who support involvement and those who reject involvement both use Vietnam as a model.

   _____

_____

_____

Exercise ———————————————————————————————

Combine the simple sentences below. Choose which idea you want to stress most, and put it into the main clause. Reduce clauses to phrases wherever possible.

1. Writing for the school paper can give students superb practical experience as journalists. The time required to work on the school paper may cost students admission to Berkeley. This is a stiff price to pay.

_____

_____

_____

_____

2. The students of the '60s believed that they could overcome all obstacles to realizing their dreams of freedom, equality, and peace. The students of the late '70s and early '80s believed that they could achieve no lasting social reform.

_____

_____

_____

_____

3. The physical and psychological effects of teenage pregnancy are formidable. Society can no longer depend on church or family to educate the young about sex. Schools should be required by the federal government to give a compulsory sex education course in the ninth and tenth grades.

_____

_____

_____

_____

_____

_____

Exercise ———————————————————————————————

Revise the point sentences below to indicate more clearly the logical relationships between their clauses and phrases.

Unclear: To present a new play on Broadway is tremendously expensive, and Broadway seldom puts on new plays, and new young playwrights are deprived of the opportunity to have their plays produced on Broadway.

Revised: Because of tremendous expense, Broadway seldom puts on new plays, and thus deprives new, young playwrights of the opportunity to have their plays produced there.

1. Some students consistently do poorly, and grades do not serve as a means of motivation and encourage them to give up.

    _____

    _____

2. Most modern-day athletes believe running to be a purely beneficial way of improving their physical fitness, and few are aware of the common leg injuries and sometimes fatal heart diseases which may ensue.

    _____

    _____

    _____

3. The Olympic Games should be a contest between the very best athletes of different nations, and the best athletes should be allowed to compete, whether they are amateur or professional.

    _____

    _____

    _____

4. Pornography is legally protected by Article I of the Constitution, which guarantees freedom of speech and of the press, and it should be illegal because it exploits women.

    _____

    _____

    _____

5. Nuclear reactors and power have been proven a safe method of providing electricity cheaply, and many people still insist the reactors are bombs.

    _____

    _____

    _____

Point Sentence Evaluation

Look at the checklist on the next page. Evaluate the following point sentences. After each sentence write the word or phrase which lists the criteria which they fail to meet. Compare your answers with those listed under Commentary.

1. Does the point sentence capture your own **interest**? Do you want to write about it?
2. Will the point sentence seem **significant** or important to your reader? Will your reader want to read on?
3. Does the point sentence express a **point of view**, a judgment or an opinion on your topic?
4. Is the point sentence appropriate in **scope**, or is its focus too broad or too narrow?
5. Is the point sentence **clearly stated**? Are its **key terms** precise, or are they vague, general, or overly abstract?
6. If the point sentence has more than one clause, are the parts of the sentence **logically connected**.

1. A good education is the greatest gift a society can give to its youth.
2. There are both advantages and disadvantages to having a job after school.
3. Students should learn different things so as to be well-rounded.
4. Almost one in four children in America is poor.
5. Supposedly grown-up men shouldn't be paid hundreds of thousands of dollars to play silly and violent games like football and hockey.
6. Because federal drug enforcement officers risk their lives to stop illegal drug trafficking, the United States should adopt mandatory drug testing programs.

COMMENTARY

1. The *scope* of sentence #1 is far too vast for adequate treatment in one paragraph. The writer needs to think of one illustration that might narrow and sharpen such a sweeping generalization.
2. The *list* promised in sentence #2 fails to make a *point*. After he discovers all the advantages and disadvantages of working after school, the writer needs to draw a conclusion that he can then express in one, clear sentence.
3. The *key terms* in sentence #3, *different things* and *well-rounded*, are so vague and general that they may condemn the writer's paragraph to broad, imprecise observations. The writer could make a more forceful point from the start if he simply narrowed and sharpened those key terms.
4. The *fact* stated in sentence #4 on its own does not make a *point*. The writer needs to interpret the fact. He must draw a conclusion that reveals the significance of the fact to him. He must indicate his point of view about the fact.
5. The *point of view* expressed in sentence #5 through such words as *supposedly* and *silly* discredits the writer's point by overstating it. The writer's point of view must be reasonable as well as clear.
6. The *because* in sentence #6 makes an *illogical connection* between the idea that officers risk their lives and the idea that testing programs should be justified. *Because* asserts a cause and effect relationship where none exists.

Exercise ————————————————————————————————————

Using the checklist on page 39, evaluate the following point sentences. Not all the sentences are weak.

1. TV is a wasteland.
2. The Battle of Little Big Horn led to the destruction of the elite Seventh Cavalry one hot June afternoon in 1876.
3. Automation has been increasing unemployment.
4. The new Official High School Basketball Rule that requires coaches to remain seated has successfully given the game back to the players.
5. Socializing has both good and bad effects on students.
6. The U.S. as a superpower has the responsibility to aid other countries because if it doesn't it will lose the respect of the less powerful nations and thus create conflict.
7. People think that protectionism is the answer to America's economic woes, but they're wrong.
8. Terrorists blow up things, kill people, or seize hostages.
9. Before rushing to package their products in tamper-proof containers, manufacturers ought to consider the elderly and the handicapped, who already have great difficulty opening their medicines.
10. Many Americans are interested in status things like expensive cars and designer clothes because they believe it improves their social standing.

Exercise ————————————————————————————————————

Revise three of the weak point sentences from the list above. Study the sample revisions below before you begin.

Original: The Super Bowl is a lot of fun.

Revised: The Super Bowl provides competition for serious football players, entertainment for serious spectators, and parties for serious partiers.

Original: Everyone should observe Martin Luther King's birthday.

Revised: The anniversary of Martin Luther King's birthday should be observed in schools by programs designed to educate students about the history of civil rights in America as well as about present-day race relations.

Original: A lot of people think that graffiti is just vandalism, but it's more than that.

Revised: Graffiti is more than just writing on empty wall space: it is a distinctive, vibrant, and sometimes angry means of expression.

4. Support the Point Sentence

In the preceding pages you have learned how to discover what you can write about by *brainstorming* and by *observing*. And you have practiced *categorizing* information in ways that have led you to draw conclusions.

You have also learned the importance of focusing on one significant conclusion in a *point sentence* that meets all the requirements for clarity and interest discussed in the last section. Like a seed that contains the genetic code for growing an entire plant, a good point sentence contains the "code" for writing an entire paragraph. Now you can concentrate on the fourth main step in the writing process: *developing the support* for your point.

The body of a paragraph is designed to support the main idea by explaining it fully and by providing examples that clarify it. All the details that helped you to draw your conclusion in the first place can now be used to support that conclusion. Not just any kind of support will do, however. The support in a fully-developed paragraph has three main characteristics: *concreteness*, *order*, and *purpose*. In the following section you will learn first how to recognize each of these characteristics and then how to write paragraphs that possess them.

Concreteness

The two paragraphs below develop this point sentence: **Trying to overcome the physical pain sustained in violent weekly games and to prolong the thrill of stardom, many professional football players use cocaine**. After reading the paragraphs, compare them by asking such questions as "Which paragraph is more interesting to read, and why? Which paragraph is more persuasive, and why?"

> Trying to overcome the physical pain sustained in violent weekly games and to prolong the thrill of stardom, many professional football players use cocaine. They receive injuries in each week's game, and these injuries take a toll. Drugs, especially cocaine, help the players mask the pain they feel. Besides making the players feel more comfortable physically, cocaine makes the athletes feel more comfortable psychologically. They can feel like a star not just on the weekend during the big game, but anytime they choose to use the drug.

Trying to overcome the physical pain sustained in violent weekly games and to prolong the thrill of stardom, many professional football players use cocaine. Each weekend's game exacts a physical toll from the players, often in the form of injuries like pulled muscles, pinched nerves, separated shoulders, or broken fingers. Cocaine helps dull the pain of the player's injuries and his general achiness because cocaine gives a feeling of well-being, even invincibility. The user feels total self-contentment and power, the same kinds of feelings a player has when he hears 80,000 fans roar their approval of a diving catch or a crucial tackle. The excitement of being a hero is addictive: the athlete longs to feel again the exhilaration and thrill he experienced from playing on national television and giving interviews to adoring sports commentators. In hiding a football player's sensations of pain and in recreating his sensations of stardom, cocaine use is quickly becoming a dangerous epidemic in professional football.

You probably agree that the second paragraph is both more interesting and more persuasive, largely because *it includes concrete details*. To show the reader why professional football players use cocaine, the writer must explain what the pain and thrill of the game are and how they push players to use drugs. *Pain* and *thrill* are broad, abstract terms with various meanings. To make the reader see his point, the writer must supply specific, concrete details that appeal to the reader's senses and stimulate his imagination, while they explain the paragraph's point. For instance, "pulled muscles," "pinched nerves," "separated shoulders," and "broken fingers" are more concrete than the word "pain." Similarly, details about the excitement of giving interviews to sports-casters, of being seen on national television, and of hearing 80,000 fans roar their approval of a diving catch or crucial tackle will draw the reader into the point about the "thrill of stardom."

Thus, specific, concrete details are used both to begin and to end the process of planning a paragraph. First, the writer brainstorms to get ideas for a point sentence, and then he brainstorms to find details to support the particular point he is making. If he writes a whole paragraph using only general and abstract terms, chances are he will bore and confuse the reader. Concrete details make the reader see and feel what he means.

Exercise

Following the example below, rank the items in each category from least to most specific.

Example: 3   vandalism
            2   street crime
            5   spray-painted obscenities on subway windows
            1   crime
            4   graffiti

_____ Chevrolet
_____ American cars
_____ modes of transportation
_____ Chevette
_____ cars
_____ cars manufactured by General Motors

_____ English springer spaniels
_____ pets
_____ dogs
_____ spaniels
_____ animals

_____ sweets
_____ Milky Way
_____ fattening foods
_____ candy
_____ food
_____ chocolate bars

_____ Cowboy running back
_____ athlete
_____ professional football player
_____ Tony Dorset
_____ Dallas Cowboy

_____ network news
_____ media
_____ CBS news program
_____ television
_____ Dan Rather's 7:00 news

_____ World War II
_____ America's participation in World War II
_____ bombing of Hiroshima
_____ participation of Army Air Corps in WWII
_____ war

Exercise ━━━

For each abstract or general term, supply a specific, concrete example. Try to be as vivid as possible.

Examples: Pain: a burning sensation in my left ear

Anticipation: cutting into the first big, plump watermelon of the season

1. furniture: _____

2. clothes: _____

3. pets: _____

4. house: _____

5. boredom: _____

6. guilt: _____

7. insecurity: _____

8. embarrassment: _____

9. food: _____

10. work: _____

Exercise ━━━

Using the poem below by Rupert Brooke as a model, write your own list of things you have loved or hated.

These have I loved:
   White plates and cups, clean-gleaming,
Ringed with blue lines; and feathery, faery dust;
Wet roofs beneath the lamp-light; the strong crust
Of friendly bread; and many-tasting food;
Rainbows; and the blue bitter smoke of wood;
And radiant raindrops couching in cool flowers;
And flowers themselves, that sway through sunny hours,
Dreaming of moths that drink them under the moon;
Then, the cool kindliness of sheets, that soon
Smooth away trouble; and the rough male kiss
Of blankets; graying wood; live hair that is
Shining and free; blue-massing clouds; the keen
Unpassioned beauty of a great machine;
The benison of hot water; furs to touch;
The good smell of old clothes; and other such—
The comfortable smell of friendly fingers,
Hair's fragrance, and the musty reek that lingers
About dead leaves and last year's ferns. . .
                          Dear names,
And thousand others throng to me! Royal flames;
Sweet water's dimpling laugh from tap or spring;
Holes in the ground; and voices that do sing;
Voices in laughter, too; and body's pain,
Soon turned to peace; and the deep-panting train;
Firm sands; the little dulling edge of foam
That browns and dwindles as the wave goes home;
And washen stones, gay for an hour; the cold
Graveness of iron; moist black earthen mould;
Sleep; and high places; footprints in the dew;
And oaks; and brown horse-chestnuts, glossy new;
And new-peeled sticks; and shining pools on the grass. . .
                       —Rupert Brooke
                   from *"The Great Lover"*

———————————————————————————

———————————————————————————

———————————————————————————

———————————————————————————

———————————————————————————

———————————————————————————

———————————————————————————

———————————————————————————

———————————————————————————

———————————————————————————

_____

_____

_____

_____

_____

Exercise ───

On separate paper, rewrite one of the two paragraphs below, using the same point sentence. Supply your own concrete details.

<u>She has a closet in the back of her mind filled with masks of different personalities and expressions.</u> Each day she puts on different masks to fit different situations. At lunch, for example, when she is with a few "intellectual" friends, her most learned mask slips on her face. Though she didn't understand *Crime and Punishment*, her mask carries on for her, throwing out ideas and pretending to follow the ideas of her friends. Later at art class, she appears as a pseudo flower child. Her slowed speech and slightly glazed eyes make her fit in perfectly with the other members of the class. But she has yet to face the most difficult challenge of the day: dinner at the cafeteria, with unfamiliar faces dominating her table. Placing on "confidence," her most reliable mask, she laughs and becomes witty and outgoing. Another successful day has passed, thanks to her masks. That night, however, as she looks in the mirror at her unmasked face, she realizes it is a face she hardly knows. She lifts her eyebrows, wondering, "Who am I really?" and goes off to sleep.

<u>The stud carefully watches himself to make sure that he is the center of attention, high above the people who surround him.</u> In the library, while everyone else reads silently, he talks and laughs, proving that *he* doesn't have to work hard. "Nerds and librarians don't faze me," he says to himself proudly. In class he shows visible disgust for students who listen to what the teacher has to say. He realizes that if those students are involved in the class discussion, they can't be thinking about him. At the school dance he struts around like Mick Jagger, feeling that he "can't get no satisfaction" because no one there is cool enough for him. In a crowd the stud is always alone. He is separated even from himself as he obsessively watches every one of his own words and actions.

Students wrote the following three paragraphs in response to the question, "How do you do your homework?" All three paragraphs do answer the question, but note how much more interesting it is to read the last two. The first writer has provided no concrete details to enliven his writing and to illustrate his points. The next two writers, however, fill their paragraphs with concrete details. Notice also that both writers have narrowed their topic: one to the way he prepares to write an English paper, the other to an extended anecdote about writing (or not writing!). Finally, notice that the last writer chose to put the point sentence at the end for emphasis.

Ideal conditions are necessary so that I may complete my homework in an efficient and organized manner. These conditions, however, vary depending upon the subject and also the assignment. For basic written work, my most productive time occurs in the library, where the quiet, undistracting atmosphere is useful. Studying, however, such as for major tests, is difficult for me to accomplish in this overly tranquil environment because it makes me too sleepy. Thus I do my cramming for tests later, after I leave the library and take a study break. In my own room, before I go to bed, I study for my tests.

Before I begin an English paper, I try to invoke a certain emotion in myself, one that matches the intended mood of my paper. I've developed an odd assortment of methods for doing this. One of my methods is to play music while I write. I play blues for sadness, Ravel's *Bolero* for intensity, Jefferson Airplane for the abstract or bizarre, Bob Dylan for quiet reflection, and the Fairport Convention for anything poetic. I've also found that certain lighting arrangements help in establishing a desired frame of mind. Sometimes I put my lamp on the floor to create strange shadows, or, for an eery red glow, I'll cover the lamp with a red cloth. Then, I sit down at my desk and try to follow the advice of the legendary sportswriter, Red Smith, who said, "All you have to do to write is to sit at a typewriter and open a vein." So I sit and wait for blood to spill. In time, it usually does.

On those all-too-frequent nights when, at midnight, an assignment for a three-page paper on the synthesis of adenine triphosphate, for example, glares at me from among my scattered notes, my conscience surrenders to my need for sleep. Only a few things appeal to me at midnight; adenine triphosphate is not one of them, so I postpone the assignment until five a.m., a blissful five hours away. However, my bliss is cut short: just as I finish snuggling contentedly into my blankets, the alarm clock suddenly assaults my ears. "So soon!" I lament, reluctantly heaving myself over to the desk, where the merciless biology topic lies in wait for me. The topic of this essay, no doubt fascinating to some, sparks no interest in a semi-conscious, puffy-eyed girl at five in the morning. Needless to say, five-fifteen finds me slumped over my desk, face resting on a page bearing only the words "adenine triphosphate is . . . ." By seven-thirty, in my dreams I'm drooling over Mel Gibson (and all over those three words in my bio notebook). Unfortunately, my tactics of "homework session at dawn" prove none too successful.

Exercise

Pretend that the place where you usually sit in the school cafeteria is already taken. You see no friends or acquaintances, only students who are strangers staring at you. If you wish, you may change the location to any other spot, say a championship basketball game, where you are frantically but unsuccessfully searching for your friends in the crowded bleachers. Write a point sentence that expresses your feelings. Then support that sentence with a paragraph full of concrete details that help the reader to feel the same emotions you are feeling.

Order

In well-developed paragraphs there is always a reason why one idea comes before or after another. All the sentences taken together form a sequence of thought and supporting details that, like stone steps across a brook, leads the reader to the writer's conclusion. Each sentence belongs in its own place. Order, that quality of arranging ideas in a sequence that helps the reader to understand your point, can be achieved in more than one way. But some kind of order is necessary if your ideas are to be understood.

Exercise

If each of the sentences in a well-ordered paragraph were to be written on a separate slip of paper and dropped into a hat, a reader should be able to take the slips of paper and reassemble the original paragraph without much difficulty. If the original paragraph was truly well-ordered, no single sentence could be placed anywhere in the paragraph but in its original position. Try to unscramble the following paragraph.

_____ He believed that because of writing, people do not commit information to memory but rather depend on external stores of writing.

_____ In the past, it aroused deep suspicion.

_____ Writing has not always been a respected way of thinking and communicating.

_____ Even worse, Plato thought, are the misreadings and misunderstandings that occur because people cannot talk with a written text and the writer is not there to explain his meaning.

_____ The ancient philosopher Plato, for example, condemned writing as an evil drug that appears to strengthen but actually weakens the mind.

Exercise

Unscramble the following two paragraphs, and discuss with your classmates how you arrived at your answers.

I.

_____ After stretching for ten seconds, the athlete should return to a relaxed position, and then repeat the exercise if desired.

_____ A static exercise involves getting into a stretch position and holding it for about ten seconds.

_____ The warm-up should begin with jogging or some other activity that will produce heat in the muscles.

_____ In sum, as long as the athlete stretches properly and does not overextend, the time and energy that stretching takes will be repaid many times over in making muscles loose and flexible and therefore ready for the strain they will undergo.

_____ The stretch should cause slight discomfort; cheating on correct form will substantially reduce the effectiveness of the exercise.

_____ Though often overlooked by young athletes, stretching should precede and follow every physical workout.

_____ Once the temperature of the muscle has been raised, a series of flexibility exercises, designed to stretch the entire body, should be performed.

_____ But on the other hand, it is essential not to overextend and run the risk of pulled or torn muscles.

_____ The most effective stretching is static—no bouncing or quick, sharp movements.

II.

_____ To express this conflict within the self, folktales, literary works, and films have used the image of the "double," either a single character divided into two antagonistic aspects, like Dr. Jekyll and Mr. Hyde in the Stevenson story, or two separate characters who have opposite qualities but who mirror each other, like Indiana Jones and his arch-enemy, Belloq, in the film _Raiders of the Lost Ark_.

_____ Although in the end, of course, good triumphs over evil, the film suggests that the villainous Belloq reflects the selfishness and unscrupulous desires in the heroic Indy.

_____ Hidden within Henry Jekyll, a wise and respected physician, are bestial impulses, which erupt when he turns into the savage, ugly Mr. Hyde.

_____ Torn between mind and body, reason and passion, social demands and instinctive desires, human nature splits and clashes with itself.

_____ Like Indy, Belloq is a daring archaeologist who is willing to take great risks on perilous adventures.

_____ Whether a character succumbs to or restrains his darker self, the double serves as a haunting image of the menacing split within human nature.

_____ Moreover, both seek the Lost Ark, and along their way pursue the same beautiful woman.

_____ Renouncing the good side of his deeply divided nature, Jekyll becomes his evil double and thus destroys himself.

_____ These two characters are the courageous, shrewd hero, Indiana Jones, and his crafty enemy, Belloq, who shadows Indy wherever he goes, thwarting the hero's valiant efforts.

_____ Instead of having one character with a dual personality, _Raiders of the Lost Ark_ portrays duality by means of two distinct characters.

How To Achieve Order

Each sentence in the preceding three paragraphs had its own place in a sequence of ideas. You were able to identify the sequence not only because the writer used obvious connectors like transitions ("on the other hand") and pronouns ("these two characters"; "Plato" . . . "He"), but also because the writer created a logical order for his ideas. In the paragraph on stretching, for example, the writer chose a _chronological_ order, beginning with what the athlete should do first and ending with what he should do last. Other useful ways to achieve order are:

spatial order: left to right; bottom to top; near to far; outside to inside
order of importance: least to most important
order of complexity: least to most complex
order of abstractness or generality: concrete to abstract; specific to general

In writing a paragraph, choose an ordering principle that suits your particular topic and point sentence. The topic itself may not necessarily suggest a particular order, but your point sentence and supporting details probably _will_ call for an appropriate choice.

Consider the topic of baseball. If you are making a point about the mounting suspense of a pitcher's no-hitter, you might organize chronologically, beginning with a brief summary of the early innings and ending with a detailed description of the final outs. But if you were describing a hitter's ideal ballpark, you might instead choose a spatial order: beginning inside and working toward the outside, you could mention the artificial turf, the nearness of the outfield wall, and air currents that carry the ball. If your point sentence discusses what makes a great shortstop, you could rank the skills in order of importance: agility, strength of arm, fielding ability, and range. Or perhaps you would like to write about the strategy of the manager. This idea could be supported by details arranged in order of complexity, from calling a bunt to making strategic use of all the players' various strengths. Finally, if your point sentence describes what makes a great all-around baseball player, you could begin with the most specific and concrete details, like physical skills, and move to more general and abstract attributes, like mental alertness, intensity, and determination.

Exercise

Using the topic "school social activities" (dances? athletic events?), imitate the model above. Write down three different ways to order information that would support three different point sentences.

_____

_____

_____

_____

_____

_____

_____

_____

_____

_____

_____

_____

_____

_____

_____

_____

_____

Exercise ————————————————————————

Write a paragraph on a topic of your choice and make it as orderly as possible. Next copy it onto 3″ × 5″ note cards, putting only one sentence on each card. Then in class exchange note cards with a partner. See whether you can put his paragraph back into its original order, and he yours. If either of you has trouble, try to revise the paragraph so that its order is clearer. Explain why you arranged your sentences the way you did. What was your ordering principle?

Exercise ————————————————————————

Each of the two point sentences below is followed by a list of subtopics that might be developed to support the sentence in a paragraph. Choose one of the sentences, think of concrete details that illustrate each subtopic, and then order your supporting material in a fully developed paragraph. Make sure that the reader can easily see how the body of the paragraph explains and provides examples that clarify the point sentence.

1. The people with whom advertising has most success are those whose lack of information makes them vulnerable.

> _Support:_ children
> people in third-world countries
> old people who live alone
> people who live in poverty

2. Advertising serves an essential purpose in our culture by reflecting and clarifying the values and goals that we all share.

> *Support:* image of beauty
> images of personal happiness
> images of success

Patterns of Development: Comparison and Contrast

Although the structure of your paragraphs should grow out of what you are trying to say, you can also learn how to express thoughts clearly by imitating *patterns of development.* You can use the pattern **comparison and contrast**, for example, when you are analyzing the significant differences and similarities between two subjects —for example, dieters who exercise and dieters who don't. Both dieters are trying to lose weight in ways that affect their stores of fat, muscle tissue, and sugar; their basic metabolism; and their feeling of fitness and well-being. But each dieter uses a different method: one exercises, the other does not. The writer uses the *block* method in the comparison and contrast paragraph below. He treats the two types of dieters in separate blocks, discussing the non-exercising dieter at length in the first half and the exercising dieter at length in the second.

Nibbling on salads and cottage cheese, the non-exercising dieter is actually much less successful than the dieter who cuts back moderately on calories and exercises regularly. At the start of his diet the sedentary dieter loses mainly water along with protein and stored sugar. This loss not only contributes to a feeling of fatigue but also makes the dieter look less fit. Moreover, the drastic reduction of calories triggers a defensive reaction in the body, a drop in the basic metabolic rate. The drop occurs because the cells are receiving less nourishment; thus, they reduce their activity to conserve energy. Because cell activity is reduced, weight loss slows down and may even stop altogether. In frustration over the minimal weight loss, the dieter often breaks his diet, with the painful result that he gains more weight than he lost. The non-exercising dieter thus faces a bleak future of tuna fish, celery, and grapefruit—and, probably, a continuing problem with overweight. The dieter who exercises regularly, however, can look forward to a life spiced with double-cheeseburgers, ice cream, and baked potatoes with sour cream. Because it is primarily fat, not sugar or muscle protein, that is burned during exercise, his weight loss may be more gradual, but is real and likely to be permanent. Building his muscle tissue through exercise, the dieter looks leaner and feels more fit. Furthermore, exercise raises his metabolism, so that his body burns calories more efficiently and more quickly, even when he is not exercising. In essence, his body's "thermostat" or "idling speed" is increased by exercise, with the result that his body will maintain a relatively stable weight, even when he has gorged on potato chips and beer. Further benefits of vigorous exercise include the suppression of appetite and the release of tensions, a process activated by the release of a natural tranquilizing chemical in the brain. Thus the dieter who exercises vigorously and regularly will lose weight, look trim, and feel healthy and fit—all without renouncing life's great taste treats.*

Now compare the *block* method paragraph with the *shuttle* paragraph written below. Here the writer shuttles back and forth between the exercising and non-exercising dieter, discussing each topic in order: what each loses, how each feels and looks, how the basic metabolism of each responds, whether each can risk an occasional splurge, and how successful overall each one is. The nature of your subject and of your details will determine which method is best for a comparison and contrast paragraph. Do you think that either of these paragraphs is more successful than the other? Why?

Nibbling on salads and cottage cheese, the non-exercising dieter is actually much less successful than the dieter who cuts back moderately on calories and exercises regularly. At the start of his diet the sedentary dieter loses mainly water, along with protein and stored sugar. This loss not only contributes to a feeling of fatigue but also makes the dieter look less fit. The dieter who exercises regularly, on the other hand, may lose pounds more slowly, but the loss is likely to be permanent because it is primarily fat, not sugar or muscle protein, that he burns during exercise. Furthermore, instead of losing muscle protein, he builds up his muscle tissue and thus looks leaner and feels better. Rather than working *with* his body as the exercising dieter does, the sedentary dieter may actually work *against* his body. As he continues to restrict his calorie intake, his body reacts defensively by dropping its basic metabolic rate. Because the cells are receiving less nourishment, they reduce their activity to conserve energy. Because activity is reduced, weight loss slows down and may even stop altogether. The exercising dieter encounters the opposite situation: exercise raises metabolism, so that his body burns calories more efficiently and more quickly, even when he is not exercising. In essence, his body's "thermostat" or "idling speed" is increased, with the result that his body will maintain a relatively stable weight, even when he has gorged on potato chips and beer. The non-exercising dieter can only dream of such feasts and, in his frustration over his slow weight loss, may break his diet and actually gain more weight than he lost because of his slowed-down metabolism. The exercising dieter feels less frustration not only because he is able to indulge occasionally, but because his appetite is suppressed and his tensions relieved by the release of a natural tranquilizing chemical in the brain. Frustrated, tired, and still overweight, the inactive dieter faces a bleak future of tuna fish, celery, and grapefruit, while the dieter who exercises vigorously and regularly will lose weight, look trim, and feel healthy and fit—all without renouncing life's great taste treats.

*Information in both paragraphs from Jane Brody, "To Lose Weight, More Exercise Is the Key," *New York Times*, 3 August 1983, pp. C1, C8.

Exercise ————————————————————————————————

Study the model point sentences below and then write three comparison and contrast point sentences of your own.

1. Although tapes and record albums both offer the same product—music—tapes appeal to less serious music lovers, while records appeal to those listeners who will gladly sacrifice convenience for high sound quality.
2. Except for bicyclists who ride long distances or who race, most people will find that a used three-speed bicycle is infinitely more practical than a new ten-speed.
3. Whereas television's "ideal male" used to be the sensitive Alan Alda-type, today's ideal man is unapologetically macho: sure of himself, unemotional, aggressive, and womanizing.
4. Boys tend to handle conflicts among themselves through physical intimidation, girls through social intimidation like gossip and exclusion.
5. _____

_____

_____

_____

6. _____

_____

_____

_____

7. _____

_____

_____

_____

Exercise ————————————————————————————————

Choose one of the seven point sentences above, and, on separate paper, write a well-developed comparison and contrast paragraph in support of it.

Cause and Effect

Cause and effect is another common pattern of paragraph development, particularly popular with historians and scientists. Using this structure, a writer might devote the paragraph to a detailed analysis of the various causes that produced one effect, or he might devote the paragraph to an analysis of the various effects of one cause. The paragraph below stresses the causes of the 1986 explosion of the space shuttle *Challenger*. It examines not only the immediate causes—technological failure and human error in deciding to go ahead with the launch despite engineers' fears—but also more remote, indirect causes such as the pressure that a blasé, over-confident public placed on NASA to perform magic tricks.

What caused the 1986 explosion of the shuttle *Challenger*? Who was to blame? We in the general public confidently assign responsibility to the mysterious "O-rings" on the solid-fuel rocket boosters and to the managers of NASA who overrode the hesitations of engineers who feared the effects of the very cold temperature that day. We are not very quick to see our own complicity in the disaster. Granted, we were not at Cape Canaveral on January 26 and we do not have any direct responsibility—much less any real understanding—of the awesome technology of the shuttle. We may not even know what an O-ring is. But we did in some indirect, remote way contribute to the whole chain of events. Our complacent expectation that American technology and know-how could make space travel simple and economical created pressure on the magicians at NASA to impress us with better and better tricks. To keep us—and Congress—on their good side and supply them with much-needed funding, NASA had to promise us not just a few launches a year, but several. And they had to show us that the shuttles could ultimately pay for themselves and even turn a profit, by carrying cargoes for different customers. The schedule, backlogged with impatient customers, took over. We were largely indifferent, paying attention only when a schoolteacher was going to join the crew. Another trick —a teacher in space. We became eager for NASA to pull this one off, and so they launched, despite the engineers' fears. But this time we weren't space conquerors, and this time we couldn't casually pat ourselves on our collective back and return to what we were doing.

In contrast to the paragraph above, which stresses the *causes* of the disaster, the paragraph below focuses on its *effects*. The cause is clear: the image of the explosion seen on television and now fixed in people's minds. Here the writer is interested in some of the *effects* that the explosion had on people's thinking.

To a nation grown accustomed to seeing NASA officials controlling their sophisticated technology from computer terminals, the explosion of the space shuttle *Challenger* with seven helpless people inside came as a shock. We had grown so used to the regularly occurring flights that the major networks did not even carry live coverage of the *Challenger* flight on January 26, 1986. But when the shuttle burst into fire, with cameras recording the agonized reactions of the crews' family and friends, our casual attitude turned to dismay and grief. There were the familiar NASA officials, still hunched in front of their computers with data marching across the screens, but the people this time were no longer in control. This time we had no vision of pilot and crew smiling into cameras as they floated weightlessly through a cockpit loaded with dials and gauges. This time we saw huge "roman-candle fuel tanks," with the small, vulnerable *Challenger* piggybacked on top. And somewhere inside that shuttle were seven people, unable to change anything. Man was not in control of machine that day; machine was in control of tiny, helpless, frail man. Paradoxically, man's power and his impotence—our creativity as well as our mortality—were revealed simultaneously to us in the spectacle of the magnificent shuttle launch that ended a minute later in a fiery death cloud.

Cause and effect can be a powerful pattern, but it is one that demands fairly strict attention to logical requirements. Make sure that you ask yourself the questions below before you jump to hasty conclusions about possible causes and effects.

1. Does the cause seem to account entirely for the effect? Or are other possible causes equally important as explanations for the effect?
2. Did the event really *cause* the effect or did the effect merely occur after the event?
3. Is it possible to *prove* that the stated cause produced the effect?

Remember that almost every effect has more than one cause, and that almost every cause has more than one effect.

Exercise ————————————————————————————————

Study the model cause and effect point sentences below and then write three of your own.

1. The "no pass-no play" rule that forbids athletes to compete unless they have a passing grade point average will spur both school officials and the athletes themselves to give academics, not athletics, top priority.
2. If students contributed more to the decision-making process in their schools, they might not only understand the reasons for rules but also feel more willing to follow them.
3. Racial and ethnic stereotypes often arise when people base their own self-esteem on the belittling of others different from themselves.
4. Reacting against the feminist movement, male television stars have recently portrayed characters who, like the detectives on "Miami Vice," are unashamedly macho.
5. _____
   _____
   _____
   _____
6. _____
   _____
   _____
   _____

7. _____

_____

_____

_____

Exercise ——————————————————————————

Choose one of the seven point sentences above, and, on separate paper, write a well-developed cause and effect paragraph in support of it.

Other Patterns of Development

In addition to **comparison and contrast** and **cause and effect**, several other traditional patterns of development can help a writer form and clarify ideas. **Definition**, one of the first and most important things a writer must do, specifies the meanings of key terms. It serves to introduce subtle or implied meanings that the writer will expand on. An **analogy** is a comparison that explains a complex point by showing how it is like a familiar experience or object. **Classification and division** increases a writer's understanding of a subject, first by dividing it into its parts and then by putting those parts into categories. Other techniques of development urge the readers to adopt a particular course of action. **Pro and con** explores the arguments for and against an issue. A writer can also describe a **problem** and offer a **solution**. A similar pattern is **means to an end**, which explains the best way to achieve a goal. These are only a few of the established methods of developing a paragraph.

Exercise ——————————————————————————

Using the terms above, identify the patterns of development used in the point sentences below. Each sentence employs a different pattern.

1. Although the definitions for the words *bachelor* and *old maid* are the same—an unmarried person—the connotations of the two words reflect an old, and still current, double standard. _____

2. Improving security precautions at airports to prevent international terrorism is like putting a Band-Aid on a bloody, infected wound. _____
_____

3. To combat teenage suicide, community health officials should train adults who have wide contact with adolescents to recognize and treat symptoms of depression. _____

4. The low-fat, high-fiber diet of many third-world countries is healthier than the typical American diet. _____

5. Even though mopeds provide inexpensive, convenient transportation, they are so dangerous that they ought to be banned from the road. _____

6. Most students who cheat fall into one of two categories: those who cheat as a matter of habit without remorse, or those who cheat out of a desperate fear of failing and suffer pangs of conscience later. _____

7. A macho "Rambo" response to international terrorism might relieve feelings of anger and victimization, but violence would merely provoke more violence from fanatical terrorists. _____

8. A carrot-and-stick approach to drunk driving, mandatory jail sentences for convicted drunk drivers and incentives for friends to forbid friends to drive drunk, would lessen the high incidence of drunk-driving fatalities.

Exercise

Write six point sentences, all on the same topic—for example, "friends" —but each using a different pattern of organization.

_____

_____

_____

_____

_____

_____

_____

_____

_____

_____

_____

_____

Purpose

In an orderly, concrete paragraph, the details still need one more trait: **purpose**. Details may be interesting in themselves, but unless you show how each one supports a point, the reader will ask, "What's the purpose of this information? Why are you telling me this? What's the point?" For example, when you write about a story or a photograph, it is not enough simply to retell the events of the plot or to describe the elements of the picture. Instead, you need to explain *how* these details support a conclusion about the story or the picture. If a detail doesn't support the point of a paragraph, it doesn't belong in that paragraph.

Same Details but Different Purposes

Take another look at the mall exercise on pages 22, 23. Notice that the two possible point sentences draw contradictory conclusions about the mall:

1. The mall offers a wide variety of experiences–bright colors, pleasing sounds, delicious tastes and smells–that stimulate customers and make them feel alive, alert, and cheerful.
2. The mall brainwashes customers, turning them into mindless robots.

Both these conclusions can be supported by some of the same details in the original paragraph. In other words, the same details can be used for two different purposes. For example, the writer could use the "security guards with two-way radios" to show how the mall gives one a sense of being watched, imprisoned, or herded. On the other hand, another writer could use the same guards to show how the mall gives one a sense of security, well-being, protection, and safety. Similarly, the "music . . . piped into the mall from several directions" could be considered mindless or soothing depending on the writer's point of view. This process of selecting details to support a point is similar to a lawyer's task: both a prosecutor and a defense lawyer must use the same facts, but each *interprets* the facts differently; each uses the facts for a different purpose.

Remember that in the writing process you must:

1. Gather details by observing and brainstorming;
2. Select details to draw a conclusion;
3. Interpret details to support an idea or conclusion.

Exercise

Read the following paragraphs about Garfield, America's favorite cat; think about the differences between them; then read the commentary.

> With his six national bestsellers, Garfield currently reigns as America's favorite cat. If Garfield desires entry to a locked room, he doesn't wait for the door to be unlocked; he kicks it down without hesitation. He can be pleasant and friendly when he wishes, but when he doesn't, he can snarl at his owner, Jon, with great ferocity. He heeds no command as he happily rips furniture and drapes, attacks mailmen and Girl Scouts, and kicks Odie, a dog belonging to Jon's friend, across the backyard. Garfield pursues his gluttonous passions, sleeping and eating, without guilt. He does all these things, yet Jon, Odie, and Odie's owner, Lyman, all tolerate him. And the public loves him!

With six national bestsellers, Garfield currently reigns as America's favorite cat because in Garfield's actions people see things they themselves would occasionally like to do but cannot. Most people, for example, would love a chance to get whatever they want, whenever they want it. Thus they cheer when Garfield kicks doors down, letting nothing stand in his way. Garfield doesn't let people stand in his way either. He is pleasant and friendly to others only when he wants to be: for instance, he alternately purrs and snarls at Jon, his owner. People, on the other hand, must always be pleasant to others, for the sake of politeness, even when they feel depressed or tired. They are bound by conscience to be considerate, unlike Garfield, who has his fun without regard for others. Garfield happily rips furniture and drapes, attacks mailmen and Girl Scouts, and kicks Odie, a dog belonging to Jon's friend Lyman. Because he has no job and doesn't care about his image, Garfield—to the envy of his fans—can sleep all day and eat all the lasagna he wants. With the thoughts and pleasures of humans but without their restrictions and responsibilities, Garfield appeals to his millions of fans by living out their secret desires.

COMMENTARY

Both paragraphs contain the same concrete details, but in the first paragraph, the details are not used to support any point. Without a point sentence as a guide, the reader wonders, "What is the writer's main idea? *Why* is he telling me that Garfield kicks down doors and rips up furniture?" The details, in other words, serve no purpose: they are not interpreted or explained.

In the second paragraph, however, the same details *do* serve a purpose: they support the point that Garfield is popular because he acts out what humans secretly would like to do themselves, but cannot. In the revised paragraph, the writer formulates a point sentence to explain *why* Garfield is popular. Moreover, he makes the purpose of every detail clear. For instance, he doesn't just mention Garfield's rudeness; instead, he *explains* that this behavior appeals to people who occasionally want to be rude themselves. Similarly, he relates Garfield's freedom to sleep and eat without restraint to his fans' wish for the same freedom. In the final sentence, the writer explains why Garfield can do what humans cannot—people have restrictions and responsibilities, while Garfield does not—and then restates the main point of the paragraph. Therefore, the writer never allows his reader to wonder "what is the purpose of this example? What is the point of this paragraph?"

Exercise

Following the pattern of the Garfield model, write two paragraphs. The first should be filled with details which have no real point. The second should be filled with the same details, but this time used in support of a more fully-developed conclusion. Make sure that you show how each detail supports the point of the second paragraph.

5. Develop the Paragraph

In the preceding pages you have learned how to recognize the three essential characteristics of well-developed paragraphs: their *concreteness*, their *order*, and their *purpose*. Now you can learn how to condense a well-ordered paragraph into a one-sentence summary of its main point. This technique is called writing a précis, a French term that literally means "a cut-down statement."*

Writing a Précis

Writing a précis is a useful mental exercise, first, because it trains you to look for the main point in whatever you read. When you take notes on your reading assignments in history or science, you are writing summaries of what the writer has said. The more you train yourself to do this, the better your reading comprehension will become. Second, writing a précis will help you to find the main point in whatever you write. If you are having trouble untangling your thoughts, if you find yourself floundering in a muddy swamp of words, or surrounded by a clutter of details, or swept aloft into a foggy cloud of abstract diction and conflicting ideas: **stop what you're doing and write a précis.** Look at the muddle you've been struggling with and ask yourself, "What am I really trying to say? Can I condense all these ideas to one main thought? Can I express that idea sharply in one sentence?" Even if at best you must come up with more than one main idea, you will at least be able then to decide which ones to subordinate. The mere attempt to write a précis will help you to discover where your thinking is sloppy or vague, where you have fudged or failed to follow one train of thought to its logical conclusion. Writing a précis will help you to work through those blind spots until your ideas are much, much clearer.

Read the following paragraph. Notice how the précis has condensed the point of the paragraph into nine words.

> When the jock walks in, his presence turns every room into a weight
> room. He strains to fill the place with his self-image, rigid and artificially
> pumped up like the muscles he so devotedly works on. The eyes of other

*A précis of a piece of writing that is longer than a paragraph is usually several sentences.

60

people, fixed on him, become the mirrors that line the walls of the weight room and reflect the physique that he spends hours chiselling like the stone of a statue. Because his identity is one of hardness, strength, and inflexibility, he cannot break out of it. He obsessively puts himself on display wherever he goes, just as he goes through the same work-out routine day after day, week after week. The jock is the victim of his own external identity; he is imprisoned in an iron cage, his own heavily muscled body.

Précis: The jock's assumed identity of power renders him powerless.

How to Write a Précis.

1. Read the paragraph through once. Then look up and ask yourself, "What's the main point of this paragraph? What is the single, most important idea that the author is trying to get across?" Jot down your answer. Now reread the paragraph slowly to make sure that you understand all the details in the passage. Look for key words and phrases that are repeated; they will guide you to the main idea.

2. Reread the paragraph a third time to check that your sense of the whole remains the same now that you have a more thorough grasp of the details. Modify your original impression if necessary. Make sure that you understand which point the author emphasizes, which points he or she subordinates.

3. Now pretend that you are the writer of the original paragraph and that you've been asked to summarize your point. Pretend that you must send your summary in a telegram that will cost you twenty-five cents a word. Adopt the author's viewpoint, but don't use his or her exact words. Use your own. A précis is not merely a series of phrases lifted from the original paragraph; it is the original distilled. Make sure once again that you understand the relationship between the *details* of the paragraph and its *ideas*. Give ideas the emphasis that the author intended.

4. Revise your précis sentence so that it is both graceful and economical. The goal is to make the fewest words carry the greatest meaning. Strive to be clear, direct, and concise. Remember, each word will cost you at least twenty-five cents.

Exercise

After reading the following paragraph, write a précis that could serve as its point sentence. (Notice the point sentence does not come first.)

The Beatles and the Rolling Stones both came from England and were probably the most important and authoritative bands of the '60s.

———————————————————————————————

———————————————————————————————

———————————————————————————————

While the Beatles were originally street kids from Liverpool who quickly became "nice boys," amiable, funny, exuberant jokers, the more middle-class Stones took on the personae of tough street kids, the "bad boy" image. As the Beatles sang about love in songs like "I Wanna Hold Your Hand" and "She Loves You," the Stones sang instead about sex, in songs like "Under My Thumb" and "Let's Spend the Night Together." While the Beatles' world view was generally peaceful, even sometimes Utopian, as in "All You Need is Love," the Stones' lyrics depicted a world of violence, conflict, and death. Accordingly, their songs about drugs, for instance, suggested bad trips—"Nineteenth Nervous Breakdown"—while the Beatles' trips seemed primarily to be good ones, as in "Lucy in the Sky with Diamonds." The Beatles were like children, blithely singing about the pleasures of life; the Stones, their hard-driving adult counterparts, were contemptuous and rebellious in a world that had grown mean.

Exercise

After reading the following paragraph, an excerpt from an essay called "The Pressure of the Group," by Joyce Maynard,* write a précis that could serve as the paragraph's point sentence.

_____

_____

_____

The presence of the group was frightening, their judgments quick and firm and often damning, and the tightness of the circle when I was in it only made the times when I was outside seem more miserable. The hierarchy was reestablished a hundred times a day—in choosing partners for science experiments, in study halls, when the exchange of homework problems began, and at lunch. But most of all in note-passing. We rarely needed to take notes, and so we passed them. We could have whispered easily enough, of course, or remained silent. (It wasn't ever that we had important things to say.) But note-passing was far more intriguing, spy-like. . . . Most of all, note-passing was exclusive. Whispers were impermanent and could be overheard. Notes could be tightly sealed and folded, their journeys followed down rows to make sure none was intercepted along the way. Getting a note, even an angry one, was always a compliment. Whenever I received one, I was amazed and grateful that I had made some slight impression on the world, that I was worthy of someone's time and ink. There were kids, I knew, whose letters died, like anonymous fan mail, unanswered and unread.

WORDINESS AND REVISION

Imagine that you're faced with a seven-hour hike straight up a mountainside and that you alone must carry everything necessary for the trip. Naturally, you will want to pack your knapsack very carefully, removing all excess baggage. You may decide to keep some heavy things like a can of pork and beans, because you know how good they'll taste at the top even though they're a nuisance to carry. So you throw out two or three packets of freeze-dried seaweed and keep the beans. But in spite of exceptions, you still must think carefully about each ounce you pack.

So it is with writing. Ask yourself about every word or phrase in your sentence, "Can I do without this?" "Do I really need this?" "Have I already said this?" "Can I say this with fewer words?" "How can I get the hardest, leanest sentence that is still comfortable, graceful, and fluent to read?"

Remember also that wordiness is not something for only you to consider. Wordiness is like adding fifty extra pounds to your reader's knapsack before you send him up the trail. He has a hard enough time getting to the top—understanding your meaning—without being weighed down by an extra fifty pounds on his back—without wading through all the unnecessary words and phrases of your sentences.

On the other hand, if you give him too few words, you'll have given him too little help along the trail—no tent, no food, no water—no essential markers. He needs enough to get by comfortably without any ambiguity or deprivation.

The revision process is aimed at achieving the goal of clear and concise sentences. Revision is largely pruning. But don't begin pruning too early in the writing process; otherwise, you will lose ideas, cut off trains of thought, and abort what might have been an original and challenging conclusion, expressed in an interesting way. Give yourself plenty of time to think of something to say, say it as freely as you can, and then spend some time pruning and revising.

Exercise

Reduce the following sentences to as few words as possible, without sacrificing any meaning.

Example: The Student Council made a determination on the proper course of action that should be followed.

Revised: The Student Council decided what to do.

1. Notwithstanding the fact that all legal restrictions on the use of firearms are the subject of heated debate and argument, it is necessary that the general public at large not stop carrying on discussion pro and con in regard to them.

———————————————————————————

———————————————————————————

———————————————————————————

2. Although we've had many breakthroughs in material for tennis rackets, the price for the rackets with those materials also are quickly becoming out of the reach of the lower classes, and I think scientists should vie for good materials without its high cost.

_____

_____

_____

3. Cigarette smokers are often people who have too much pressure, created by professional demands, children's needs and emotional problems such as insecurity, and try to relieve this intolerable pressure by having something to hold onto, as opposed to the nonsmoker who often does not have this pressure or is more secure and confident and can thus deal with this pressure.

_____

_____

_____

4. Cigarettes are often soothing and give security to a person on whom much emotional pressure is exerted daily, yet smoking can at the same time let one person know that another who smokes is possibly insecure or unconfident, thus often lowering one's opinion of the other, for example, on a job interview.

_____

_____

_____

5. Because cigarette smoking often causes cancer or lung disease, which are often fatal, there could be higher tax on cigarettes and more influence on the hazards of cigarette smoking, which together would discourage smoking.

_____

_____

_____

6. The nuclear freeze is a more important issue than taxation or the state of the economy because nuclear freeze is a potentially life-saving issue; therefore, during elections it should be the most important if not the only issue considered.

_____

_____

_____

Point, Précis, and Opening Sentences

A point sentence is merely a précis of a paragraph that has not yet been written. It contains the substance of the paragraph distilled: its point. A précis is a one-sentence summary of a paragraph that has already been written. Thus, the précis and point sentence are virtually the same things.

Starting a paragraph with a point sentence helps give beginning writers control over supporting ideas and details by expressing the essence of the paragraph at the start. Later, after they've fully mastered the principles of concreteness, order, and purpose, they can start to use opening sentences that capture the reader's attention while implying or withholding the point. More advanced writers often save their conclusions until the end of their paragraphs, building up to a point of emphasis.

If beginners write opening sentences that are not point sentences, they may sacrifice the clarity and control that point sentences offer. Therefore, until they've mastered each step of the writing process, they should continue to start their own paragraphs with point sentences and to write one-sentence précis of other people's paragraphs. The time and effort it takes to master these skills will pay off in the long run by enabling students to write more efficiently and easily.

Opening Sentences

To understand the difference between a good opening sentence and a good point sentence, study the example below:

Opening: Already victimized by a disease that causes steady deterioration and inevitably early death, children with AIDS must face the added burden of being feared and rejected.

Point sentence: As long as they are healthy enough to participate in the normal school routine, children with AIDS should be allowed to attend public school.

Notice that the opening sentence doesn't tell the reader what the author's conclusion will be, but does introduce the topic of the paragraph in a way that gently encourages the reader to continue reading.

Below are some more examples of good opening sentences that are not, however, good point sentences because they do not summarize the main idea of a paragraph. Discuss them with your classmates and see if you can transform them into point sentences.

1. Although soap operas are full of many depressing things like divorce, death, illness, infidelity, and violence, millions of people sit down to watch them every day.

2. Twenty years ago, eating disorders like anorexia and bulimia were almost unknown; today these seem almost as common as the flu.
3. The only sin in espionage is getting caught. (Richard Helms, former Director of the CIA.)
4. Never much of a strategist or tactician, General George Custer, nevertheless, was known to the public and to his officers as a lucky man.

Sometimes a startling fact makes a particularly good opening sentence:

1. Almost one in four children in America is poor.
2. Ninety percent of Americans think they weigh too much.
3. Prisons have nearly doubled their population since 1970.

Some sentences, and these are the ones you should strive to write, are both good point sentences and effective openers. Look at the examples below:

1. Already victimized by a disease that causes steady deterioration and inevitably early death, children with AIDS are again cruelly and this time unnecessarily victimized when they are deprived of their right to attend school.
2. Twenty lawyers with subpoenas will not be able to stop one terrorist with a machine gun and a sack of hand grenades.
   This sentence on terrorism not only grabs the reader's attention but also suggests the paragraph's main point—that reciprocal force, not legal action, is the only defense against the violence of terrorism.
3. Prisons are factories that produce criminals: convicts are worse when they get out than when they went in.
4. Being "cool" means working very hard to appear not to be working hard.

The Middle Ground

Remember that the best point sentences strike a middle ground between being overly general and excessively detailed. Sweeping generalizations offer writers no help when it comes to focusing their thoughts or ordering their information. On the other hand, an excessively detailed point sentence threatens to cram all the information of the paragraph into one sentence that leaves nothing for the reader to learn. The one offers no help, the other no surprises. Therefore, head for the middle ground of generalization between these two extremes. And if you must lean to one side, do so in the direction of greater specificity, at least while you are still a beginner.

Puffed versus Developed Paragraphs

Just as one can condense a whole paragraph to a précis, so one can take a précis and develop a whole paragraph from it. But *to develop* does not mean *to puff up*. To develop means to write a detailed, orderly, and purposeful paragraph. To puff up means to repeat the same generalization four or five times in slightly different words. The writer does this usually because he hasn't spent enough time thinking concretely about the topic: he hasn't gathered specific ideas and details. Instead, he hopes to fill space with as many words as he can so that the finished piece will look like a developed paragraph. In fact, it's only puffed.

MODEL PUFFED PARAGRAPH

      Though everybody in America seems to watch TV, television is not really very influential after all is said and done. People spend countless hours a day in front of their TV sets, but a great deal of time spent with television does not necessarily mean that it has a great deal of influence. The television is supposed to have taken over people's homes and lives, to have usurped their minds and bodies and souls. It's supposed to be the center of everything in the house now. Everybody is supposed to have nothing better to do all day long but watch endless hours of television. All the time you hear about how people claim that TV has a negative influence on people, but it doesn't really. How can it? Strictly speaking, people just don't pay that much attention to it. And besides TV can't influence everybody the same way if everybody watches different shows all the time. All in all, TV does not have the powerful influence it is supposed to have.

To rewrite a "puffed" paragraph, first write a précis of it to discover the main idea—if there is one.

Précis: Television is not as influential as it seems to be.

Next, ask yourself the question(s) raised by the point sentence, and collect specific, concrete answers. Then order those answers. Finally rewrite the paragraph to support the précis.

Question: Why is TV not so influential as it seems to be? What limits its influence?

Answers: —People do something else while TV is on.
          —Television picture doesn't hold attention.
          —Other sources of news limit the influence of TV news.
          —People limit TV's influence by shutting off bad shows, turning on good shows.

MODEL DEVELOPED PARAGRAPH

      Though found in almost every home in America, television is not as influential as it seems to be. First, although people spend six or seven hours a day in front of their TV sets, they frequently do other things at the same time: talk, eat, read, or sleep. Therefore, they seldom concentrate their attention on the television and may even completely ignore it for most of the time it is on. Second, the television's picture itself will not hold their attention. The small, square screen makes images appear distant, boxed in, unrealistic—unlike the wide screen in a movie theatre, which creates a direct and powerful connection between audience and image. Third, although television news may evoke a strong response, that happens simply because the stories are real, not because they are conveyed by the medium of television. Moreover, TV does not monopolize the news. People also turn to many other sources of information—newspapers, magazines, books, personal experience—which give the impression of being more accurate and thorough because they do not reduce all events to sixty-second spots. Finally, just as people are selective about the source of their news, so they are selective about the programs they watch. They do not sit down in front of the tube like robots and allow it to control their minds. They exercise critical intelligence in choosing shows, quickly distinguishing what is good from what is not. The good shows survive, as long as they maintain their high standards, while the bad ones die a swift and well-deserved death. Thus television does not control its viewers; rather, they limit its power in several direct and indirect ways.

Exercise

Write a précis of the following "puffed" paragraph on friendship. Then develop the précis in your own orderly, concrete, and purposeful paragraph.

True friendship involves many things, but one thing it most certainly does not involve is flattery. The worst kind of friend to have is the kind of friend who flatters you all the time. Flattery is excessive, insincere praise. A false friend gives you praise when you don't deserve to be praised, making it insincere. Few things can hurt a guy more than to be praised when he doesn't deserve it. A true friend would never flatter his friends because he would know that's the quickest way to hurt his "friends." In conclusion, a true friend never praises someone insincerely, because only false friends flatter.

Précis: _____

_____

Question: _____

_____

_____

_____

Answers: _____

_____

_____

DEVELOP THE PARAGRAPH ——————— **69**

Developing Paragraphs from Point Sentences

Wasting your reader's time with "puffing"—unnecessary repetition and redundancy—is one thing. But taking time to support a point with several good examples or to explain a difficult point thoroughly is another. The following technique may help you to develop rather than puff a paragraph from a point sentence. First, put boxes around the key terms of the sentence.

Example: Having moved from stereo to video, rock groups in the '80s emphasize their appearance, not their sound.

Next ask yourself, what questions will I have to answer in my paragraph if I am going to explain and develop each of these key terms? Write the questions down and then jot down any answers that occur to you.

Questions: Which rock groups? Can you provide any examples?
Answers: Motley Crue, Madonna, Michael Jackson

Questions: How do they emphasize their appearance?
        How do they play down their sound?
Answers: Motley Crue
        Appearance: dirty hair; dog collars; boots; gold teeth
        Sound: dull variations on three chords
        Madonna
        Appearance: racy black lace
        Sound: nobody watches her for that
        Michael Jackson
        Appearance: one glove; great dancer
        Sound: doesn't even write his own songs

Now you're ready to write a draft of your paragraph. Remember to begin and end with variations on the point sentence so that the main idea will stay firmly in your reader's mind.

MODEL PARAGRAPH

Rock music in the '80s is something worth seeing, but not worth listening to. Because the main medium for rock music has changed from stereo to video, rock groups in the '80s put more stock in their appearance than they do in their music. Therefore, the only truly innovative and exciting element of most groups today is the way they look, not the way they sound. For example, take one of the hottest selling genres of rock today, heavy metal. Guys in bands like Motley Crue grow their hair down long and dirty, wear dog collars and leather boots, and sneer into the camera, revealing three gold teeth. Now that's interesting. Their music, however, is about as dull as it can be—just variations on the three great power guitar chords. Another big seller of the '80s is Madonna. Many of the girls who go to her concerts, the "Wanna Be's," dress up in Madonna's racy style of black lace. But how many of them bring guitars and sing her songs in the parking lot before the concert? If you want to be like Madonna, all you have to do is dress up, not be able to sing or play an instrument. It's the same with Michael Jackson. When you think of the "Thriller" superstar, you think of a fantastic dancer who wears one glove. You don't think about his music—he doesn't even write all of his own songs. He spent ten million dollars on his video "Thriller," but he had someone else write the song for him. These rock stars aren't unusual; many groups today are so dependent upon their video images that they bring huge TV screens to their concerts —two of them, sometimes—so that the audience has only to watch, not necessarily listen. If you turn the volume off on the music of the '80s, you're still getting the whole picture.

Exercise

Put boxes around the key terms in each of the following point sentences. Then choose three of the sentences, and write down the questions which you would have to answer if you were going to write paragraphs supporting them.

Example: [Recent proposals] to combat [espionage with lie detector tests] and [drug abuse with mandatory drug tests] threaten [Fourth Amendment freedoms.]

> What are the recent proposals?
> Who has proposed them? For what groups of people?
> What are Fourth Amendment freedoms?

Example: [America's homeless] lead an [invisible life on the street] while they [struggle] each day [to stay warm, dry, and fed.]

> Who are America's homeless?
> What is their life on the street like? Why is it invisible?
> Do they manage to stay warm, dry, and fed, and how?

1. By looking at a teenager's clothes, one can learn about that individual's personality.
2. Homosexual couples who live together deserve the same work benefits as heterosexual couples.
3. Americans should buy foreign cars until domestic cars become more reliable, efficient, and economical.
4. The new Official High School Basketball Rule that requires coaches to remain seated has successfully given the game back to the athletes.
5. The United States must be able to deal with terrorists as brutally and as deviously as terrorists themselves deal with the United States.
6. It is skill, training, and motivation that determine winners.

_____

_____

_____

_____

_____

_____

_____

_____

_____

_____

Exercise

The key terms in the following point sentence have been put into boxes. Now ask yourself, "What questions will I have to answer in my paragraph if I am going to explain and develop each of those terms?" Write the questions below, and scribble down any answers that occur to you on the spot.

[Violence] that often occurs [in physical-contact sports] tends to [spur aggression] [off the field.]

Questions: _____

_____

_____

_____

Now use any of the pieces of information listed randomly below, or any information that you have from your reading or your experience, to answer the questions. Then write an orderly, concrete, and purposeful paragraph supporting the point sentence.

Random list of details*

An increase in amount of violence among sports fans in recent years.

Fans say increased violence reflects increasingly violent society in general.

Researchers say fans imitate violence on field when sport is especially brutal and angry; fans follow example of players when inhibitions lowered by excitement, anonymity, drinking.

American researcher (Jeffrey Goldstein, of Temple University) says American football "teaches and stimulates violence"; football increases aggression of players and of some fans.

Baseball has the greatest number of such incidents: not much body contact but lots of violent moments: bean balls, fights with umpires, broken-up double plays.

*Information from _International Herald Tribune_, September 6, 1985.

Football, basketball, ice hockey, boxing—all follow close behind.

Latin America incidents occur when furious fans storm the field to attack a ref who has made an unpopular call.

British soccer seems to be the worst: blamed for 38 deaths and 200 injuries at Brussels in spring of '85. Caused by young men, 17–24 yrs. old, engaging in "aggro," form of ritualized angry confrontation, a mixture of bluff and macho posturing. People killed because stadium wall collapsed by accident after British fans were bluffing Italians to stay away from their "territory."

In Australia rowdiness breaks out at cricket matches.

Strong differences from culture to culture in what triggers sports violence and what form it takes.

Most fans are peaceful; a "youthful minority" accounts for almost all incidents of violence off the field.

People used to think that aggressive sports contained violence for both player and watcher: relieved frustration; let off steam; defused aggression.

Some even argued that international games like the Olympics could substitute for war.

Now researchers say the evidence doesn't support this theory.

Developing Paragraphs from Generalizations

Developing a paragraph from a point sentence is a fairly straightforward process. However, developing a paragraph from a generalization poses special problems for the writer. Read the following paragraphs written on the generalization "Growing up requires the acceptance of limitations."

1. In order to grow up, one must accept the physical and moral limitations that will be placed on him during his growing period. He must learn to live with the boundaries that he or someone else will make for him. He has to accept certain things as being right, and try to adhere to them. If a person can do this, he (or she) will grow up to be a mature, responsible adult.

2. Sometimes a baby seems like all lungs and mouth. When he is not being fed, he is shrieking to be fed. He wants to rule over his world like an all-powerful king or god, insisting that his parents pay homage to him by instantly satisfying his every need and desire. Yet the baby soon discovers that he does not have supreme control, that his parents do not exist solely for his sake. Because they have their own needs and desires, they cannot come running every time he cries. He thus learns that immediate gratification is not always possible. A realistic view of life requires that he limit his demands and accommodate himself to other people. Therefore, even the earliest stage of human development involves the acceptance of limitations.

Notice that both writers make the same point, that growing up *does* require the acceptance of limitations. But whereas the second writer has narrowed his focus to one concrete example (the change in a baby's expectations about the world) to prove his point, the first writer does not focus his answer at all: he repeats basically the same idea four different times, without supplying any concrete details to illustrate and support his assertion. What *are* the physical and moral limitations placed on growing people? What *are* the boundaries he mentions? What *are* the certain things that are right? Without specific details to explain what his generalizations mean, the first writer makes his point neither persuasive nor interesting.

Remember, therefore, when you write about a generalization, first narrow its scope. Limit the broad statement so that you will, in fact, be developing your own point sentence. It is particularly important to master this skill if you plan to take any of the College Board essay tests.

Exercise

Write a paragraph on one of the following generalizations. Narrow its focus to one, two, or three concrete examples that illustrate and support your point.

1. A good example is the best sermon. (Ben Franklin)
2. Diplomacy is the art of letting someone else have your way.
3. 80% of life is just showing up or making an appearance. (Woody Allen)
4. I wouldn't want to be a member of any club that would have me as a member. (Groucho Marx)

Developing Paragraphs from Direct Observation

Now that you've had some practice developing paragraphs from point sentences and from generalizations, try once again to write about something that you observe directly. The photograph on page 75 was taken by a student. Given the question, "What effect does this photograph create?", the writer first made a list of concrete details and impressions, then categorized that list, and finally drew one main conclusion about the photo's effect. The paragraph on page 77 supports that conclusion. After you have studied the model, try following the entire process yourself as you answer the same question about the student photograph on page 78.

DETAILS OBSERVED AND IMPRESSIONS CREATED

foreground looks like a landing strip
eerie, cold, ghostly
deserted bleachers; game's over; emptiness

two lights are the most puzzling part of photo; they seem related to each
   other

overall, a lunar landscape

the large, steaming, white blob overwhelms the center of the picture;
   could the moon have made that light?

drizzly night, steam and fog

snow plow has piled up snow banks on sidelines

tree faintly visible behind bleachers

house or building with lighted windows barely visible to left of blob

mysterious source of smaller light shining through bleachers, from a
   house?

a lunar landing with no witnesses, no one there to greet the aliens, no
   one to be awed or terrified

no humans in the picture—only empty bleachers

alien touching down on an empty playing field at night, signalling to
   another alien behind the bleachers; two parallel blobs; invasion of the
   body snatchers

lights on in the house; somebody must be at home

ball of steaming vapors like a full moon on a stormy night, but too large
   and too close to earth to be the moon; fireworks? no; what is it? can't
   tell

football field seems as vast as a moonscape or the alkaline flats of Nevada
   desert at night

banks of plowed snow look like miniature Rocky Mountains, rough and
   jagged peaks, rising out of the flats

frozen, smooth path of ice on the field like a runway

Photograph by Istvan Szent-Miklosy.

CATEGORIES

Familiar, Natural Effects
> deserted bleachers on a football field at night
> drizzly night, steam and fog; ice on field
> snow plow has piled up snow banks on sidelines
> tree faintly visible behind bleachers
> house or building with lighted windows barely visible to the left of the blob
> no humans in picture, but house lights are on—somebody must be at home
> empty playing field where humans have been earlier, though gone now; emptiness after plowing, cheering, playing

Alien, Supernatural Effects
> foreground like a landing strip; frozen, smooth path of ice on the field like a runway
> distortion of normal scale: field seems much vaster than it is; moonscape, or alkaline flats of Nevada desert at night; jagged mountains rising out of the flats
> supernatural, amorphous white blob of mysterious origin dominates the photo

Mysterious Lights
> two parallel lights are the most puzzling part of photo; they seem related to each other
> The large, steaming, white blob in the center is overwhelming; could the moon have made that light? ball of steaming vapors like a full moon on a stormy night, but too close to earth and too large to be the moon. What is it? Can't tell. second, smaller light seems more natural—could be from house behind bleachers—but because it repeats the shape of the bigger blob, it too seems mysterious, related to the larger one.

PRELIMINARY CONCLUSIONS

1. Alien touching down on an empty playing field at night and signalling to another alien behind bleachers. No one there to marvel at them, no one to be awed or terrified. Spectacular, supernatural event, but no one there to watch; empty bleachers; everybody has gone home. Ironic.
2. Without the weird blob and echoing smaller blob, the picture's effect would have been forlorn, desolate, lonely—empty bleachers at night. Game's over. Sense of coldness and loss. With the supernatural, one gets an entirely different impression: loneliness has been preempted by curiosity, drama, mystery, action, spectacle, and humor.

CONCLUSION

The spectacular supernatural event in the photograph takes place at night when, ironically, no one is in the bleachers to see it. It would have been just as mysterious and funny if Neil Armstrong had found empty bleachers on the moon.

MODEL PARAGRAPH

The main effect created by Istvan Szent-Miklosy's untitled photograph on page 75 is one of mystery mixed with humor. A large, white steaming blob of mysterious origin dominates the picture and puzzles the viewer. No natural explanation seems to account for the spectacular shape. Moreover, it is not alone. A parallel blob, smaller but steaming as well, peeks through some empty bleachers on the sidelines of a lunar-looking playing field late on a winter night. Could one blob be a landing alien, signalling to its twin? The photograph guarantees its effect of mystery by refusing to offer the viewer any easy answers. But mystery alone will not explain the picture's complete effect, for the longer one looks at the bleachers, the more ironic it seems that no one is there to witness this spectacle. Human activities such as plowing snow, playing sports, and cheering teams are over; all spectators have gone home for the night. How funny to have missed the most astonishing drama of all. Without the mysterious, supernatural blobs, the photograph would have seemed forlorn, desolate, and lonely. The viewer might have felt a sense of coldness and loss, now that the game was over. Instead, the picture surprises the viewer with the drama and humor of a possible alien landing. The spectacular event recorded in the photograph goes unwatched, in spite of the bleachers. If Neil Armstrong had found empty bleachers on the moon, it would have been as mysterious and funny.

Exercise ————————————————————————————————————

Review the process on the previous five pages. Observe concrete details from the photo below. Categorize them and write a point sentence. Then choose the details which support your point sentence and develop a paragraph.

Photograph by Martin Meyer.

6. Improve Coherence

Coherence comes from the Latin word meaning "to stick together." Each part of a coherent paragraph sticks to every other part of the paragraph to form a seamless whole. You have already studied in detail the most important means of achieving coherence: arranging the sentences of a paragraph in a logical order or pattern, whether of similarity and difference, cause and effect, general to specific, or least to most important. Paragraphs that have a particular design or structure are usually coherent.

In the preceding section you learned that certain patterns of organization can save a writer time when he arranges his ideas. Similarly, certain structural and stylistic techniques can help a writer to improve the coherence of a paragraph already coherent in thought. You can master these techniques just as you would learn rules for correct punctuation. Remember, however, that the coherent thought must come first. Trying to "fix up" a radically incoherent paragraph is like trying to dress up a basically flabby body. If your thoughts are in good shape from regular writing practice and exercise, and if your supporting details are vivid and relevant, then these techniques will help you to polish the surface of your prose. Study the five techniques for achieving coherence listed below.

1. Repeat key words and phrases, or use synonyms.
2. Repeat parallel grammatical forms.
3. Keep tenses consistent.
4. Keep a consistent point of view.
5. Use transitional words or phrases.

Repeat Key Words and Phrases

You will help a reader to follow your thoughts by repeating key terms and phrases throughout your paragraph. You must do this skillfully so that you don't lose the reader's interest with monotonous repetition. Keep the main idea of the paragraph firmly in your reader's mind with closely related words that reinforce that idea. Notice how the writer of the paragraph below achieves coherence by repeating words that describe the cost of smoking: "high price," "pay," "paying," "expense," "costs," "expense," "costly," "ill afford."

Although many people find smoking satisfying, they don't realize the high price they pay for that satisfaction. A pack of cigarettes sells for a dollar, and heavy smokers can end up paying as much as $700 a year to support their habit. They will argue that the pleasure they derive from cigarettes is worth the expense, but it's not just money that goes up in smoke. Their habit costs them friends. As they puff away contentedly, producing thick, noxious clouds of smoke, they don't consider the people around them, who are coughing, wheezing, and rubbing their bleary eyes. Worst of all, smokers indulge their habit at the expense of their own health. Cancer and heart disease are two costly effects of cigarettes. If smoking is a pleasure, it's one that most people can ill afford.

Exercise

In the paragraph below put boxes around key words and phrases that the writer repeats to reinforce his main point.

To be successful, an athlete needs complete physical fitness, which involves cardiovascular conditioning, muscular endurance, strength, and flexibility. A carefully planned weight training program, repeated three times a week, will help the athlete improve in all these elements of physical fitness. If performed with minimal rest between exercises, weight training makes the heart pump faster and harder and thus contributes to cardiovascular endurance. It also improves the endurance of the muscles, so that the athlete will be able to persist in strenuous muscular activity for a longer period of time. The athlete will have the capacity to perform not only longer but also more forcefully because weight training increases strength as well. A stronger athlete will be more explosive, more confident, and less susceptible to injury. Flexibility, like strength, decreases the severity and number of injuries; and here, too, weight training done properly and combined with thorough stretching, is beneficial. It strengthens the muscles around the joints, which thereby become more resilient. For the athlete who is committed to increasing endurance, bettering performance, and reducing injury, a demanding weight training program is essential.

Repeat Parallel Grammatical Forms

The following words, phrases, and clauses are all examples of parallel structure:

The American League's designated hitter rule is better for the *fans, teams,* and *players* than the National League's traditional rule. (Words are parallel.)

The school president promises *to improve the school lunches, to eliminate detention, and to increase faculty awareness of student fatigue and anxiety.* (Phrases are parallel.)

Sue is interested in the field of computers, *which is a booming industry* and *which offers a wide variety of interesting jobs.* (Clauses are parallel.)

Readers will understand your points much more easily and quickly when you use parallel grammatical forms to express parallel ideas. Such a style can improve the coherence of your paragraphs dramatically.

Exercise

Boxes have been drawn around the first two parallel forms in the two paragraphs below. Draw boxes around the remaining parallel structures.

My English Bulldog, George, has a finely-developed sense of his prerogative. In fact, George really believes that he isn't a dog at all, but a human. When I am eating dinner, he growls with annoyance and waits with a sense of injured pride until I move his food bowl to a spot on the floor right next to my chair. Whenever I am tardy, lax or neglectful, George's reprisals follow instantly. Picking only those objects that he knows I want intact, he destroys them. So far this year he has devoured *War and Peace; Look Homeward, Angel; Rabbit, Run*, and the Boston telephone directory. At least he has good taste. Though I tried to instill some principles of rank and hierarchy into his flat, thick, little head, he remains resolute: George just doesn't appreciate that I'm supposed to be the master and he's supposed to be the obedient, submissive, and slavishly-devoted hound.

And after all, life on a blue bag under the kitchen table is not bad; one could do much worse. Perhaps it is understandable that he trundles through each day with an unmistakable air of self-satisfaction. In fairness, George does have a kind heart and a gentle soul even though he looks ferocious and behaves at times like a tyrant. For all his exasperating sense of entitlement, he would never do anything mean-spirited or sly. And because he has such staying power, I have slowly begun to see things his way. Though I'm not sure whether he has risen to the level of human or I have sunk to the level of bulldog, I suspect that the Lord, in fact, made all his creatures equal and that I have just been slow to see George's point.

Keep Tenses Consistent

Example: "He worked hard on the paper, but receives only a 'C'."

Revision: ". . . received only a 'C'."

Exercise

The following paragraph contains four lapses in correct verb tense. Put boxes around and correct the three remaining errors.

A common phenomenon of college life is the "all-nighter," the night-long attempt to catch up on academic work. But it's hard to understand the appeal and mystique of all-nighters when one considers their inevitable effects. Faced with the prospect of studying for a French quiz, finishing a lab report, and writing an English paper, students often think to themselves,

"No problem. I'll just pull an all-nighter." Having made this decision, they announce it to all their friends and dormmates, winning cries of sympathy and respect. They then ⟨ordered⟩ out, call home, and have an earnest two-hour conversation with a few close friends, all in preparation for—and justified by—their plan to stay up all night. Finally, after they have become sated with conversation, pizza, and soda, they returned to their rooms around midnight and huddle over the paper assignment. Five hours later they are still huddled over the paper—sound asleep. Awakening with a jolt, they would furiously copy over the scribbles on the page, stare uncomprehendingly at their French text, and consider excuses for the biology teacher. As they sit (or slump) through morning classes and meet the curious glances of friends, the bleary-eyed heroes smiled grimly with pride. Three days later, however, the predictable consequences of the all-nighter are known: a zero for an incomplete lab report, a 52% on a French quiz, and a "D" on the English paper, accompanied by the comment, "You must have written this in your sleep!"

Keep a Consistent Point of View

Avoid shifting from one person to another.

Example: "If ⟨one⟩ wants a career in computer science, you ⟨have⟩ a wide range of opportunities."

Revision: ". . . ⟨one⟩ has a wide range of opportunities."

Exercise

The following paragraph contains three shifts in person. Put boxes around and correct the remaining two errors.

Most high schools have cliques. As teenagers try to figure out who they are, they band together with others who are like them. For example, ⟨he⟩ may play the same sport, come from the same socio-economic class, listen to the same music, or belong to the same clubs. Together they have a clear identity: they're the "jock crowd" or the "artsy crowd" or the "popular group" But something funny happens to the members of a clique: to share the comfortable, secure identity of the group, they begin to give up much of their individual identities. To be part of the crowd you have to do and say the "right" things. They may even find themselves *thinking* what the crowd thinks. For instance, instead of making up their own minds about a new kid at school, the members might accept the judgement of the group. Or rather than deciding to pass up a drinking party after the Friday night basketball game, they each go along with the crowd. If one thinks about it, they might discover that they have given up some of their individual identities to adopt the identity of their clique.

Use Transitional Words or Phrases

Transitional words help you connect one idea to the next in your paragraph. The most superficial means of achieving coherence, transitions are like signposts on an already straight road. Transitions will not help a disorganized paragraph, but they will make a well-ordered paragraph more fluent. The reader will follow your points more easily if you use the following words:

ADDING: again, also, and, and then, besides, further, furthermore, in addition, moreover, too.

SEQUENCING: first, second, third, next, last, finally.

SUMMARIZING: in brief, in short, in conclusion.

EXEMPLIFYING: for example, for instance, in particular.

CONCLUDING: as a result, consequently, accordingly, therefore, thus, then, for, so.

OPPOSING: but, however, in contrast, nevertheless, on the contrary, on the other hand, yet, still, unlike, in spite of.

INTENSIFYING: in fact.

ALTERNATING: or, on the other hand, either.

IDENTIFYING CAUSE: because, for, since.

IDENTIFYING TIME: afterwards, immediately, in the meantime, meanwhile, soon, at least, while, presently, shortly.

Study the sentences and their revisions below to discover how transitions help the reader to follow a sequence of ideas.

1. Most older Europeans remember World War II and foreign occupation and remain committed to a fully armed NATO Defense Force. The younger generation considers a missile-armed NATO a threat to peace.

   [While] most older Europeans . . . , the younger generation . . .
   Most older Europeans . . . , [but] the younger generation. . . .

2. Hundreds of thousands have marched in Europe, many carrying anti-Reagan signs. Hundreds of thousands have marched in America. Many marched in Central Park in June '82 and some of those people carried anti-administration placards.

   . . . anti-Reagan signs. [Similarly,] hundreds of thousands have marched in America, [for example,] in Central Park in June '82. Some of those marchers carried anti-administration placards [as well.]

3. There are political effects of such broad-based protest movements. World leaders, especially Reagan, have modulated their cold-war rhetoric and have approached peace talks with more open minds.

   . . . broad-based movements; [for instance,] . . . .
   . . . . movements; [most important,] . . .
   . . . . movements; [most notably,] . . . .

Exercise ——————————————————————————————————————

The first two transitions have been put in boxes. Put boxes around at least four more.

For city commuting, used three speed bicycles are more useful than new ten-speed bicycles. With a fancy ten-speed, you must be careful when going up and down curbs, so that you don't damage the delicate aluminum rims. But because a three-speed is built like a tank, with solid steel rims, you can go over practically anything. For example, you can ride a three-speed over various road hazards like puddles, rocks, potholes, and small children without fear of damaging the bike. On the other hand, if you do happen to damage it, you can replace it for $10–$20, while even minor repairs to a fancy and fragile ten-speed cost about $50. Thus the ten-speed owner riding in the city spends half his time walking his bicycle around various obstacles, while the three-speed owner casually and efficiently rides right over them. Once he does get to work, the ten-speed owner must carry his bike into the building, and often up several flights of stairs, to protect his machine against theft. However, the three-speed owner can leave his bike outside, with a cheap lock, and nobody will find it worth stealing. Using a ten-speed instead of a three-speed bike for city commuting is like using fine china instead of a mess kit for backpacking: not only is it more expensive, but it is not nearly as practical.

7. Use an Edit Sheet

Directions: Your teacher will assign you a partner, whose rough draft you should read carefully. Then look over all the questions on this page and begin to answer them as fully as you can. If you criticize, be sure to make helpful suggestions for correcting the problem. After twenty minutes of silent work, you and your partner should discuss one another's suggestions.

Editor: _____   *Author:* _____

1. Carefully read the paragraph and state here, in your own words, its main point.

   _____

   _____

   _____

   _____

2. Underline the author's point sentence. Does it correspond with the sentence you wrote above? Revise the author's sentence if it does not accurately express the paragraph's main idea.

   _____

   _____

   _____

   _____

3. Examine the point sentence closely.
   a. Is it interesting and significant? Is the author's point of view clear? Do you want to read on? Why or why not?

   _____

   _____

   _____

   b. Is it appropriate in scope? Explain your answer.

   _____

   _____

   _____

c. Are the parts of the sentence logically connected? If not, rewrite the sentence.

_____

_____

_____

d. Underline its key terms. Are they clear, precise, and well-focused? Suggest changes if necessary.

_____

_____

_____

4. Does the author provide concrete, specific details to support the point sentence? Suggest another detail or two, or make one or two details _more_ concrete.

_____

_____

_____

_____

_____

5. Are the details ordered in a clear and logical manner? Describe the ordering principle (chronological, least to most important, cause-effect, shuttle or block comparison and contrast, etc.). Suggest an order if there isn't one.

_____

_____

_____

6. Do the details clearly support the point sentence? Do you understand the purpose of each one? List any whose purpose is unclear.

_____

_____

_____

_____

7. Is the paragraph coherent? Underline transitions, repeated key words, and any other method of achieving coherence. Suggest revisions for any sentence that isn't linked to the one coming before and after it.